Self-Sufficiency Gardening

Financial, Physical and Emotional Security from Your Own Backyard

A Practical Guide for Growing Vegetables, Fruits, Nuts, Herbs, Medicines and Other Useful Products

Self-Sufficiency Gardening

Financial, Physical and Emotional Security from Your Own Backyard

by Martin P. Waterman

A Practical Guide for Growing Vegetables, Fruits, Nuts, Herbs, Medicines and Other Useful Products

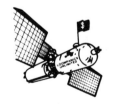

Loompanics Unlimited
Port Townsend, Washington

Self-Sufficiency Gardening: Financial, Physical, and Emotional Security from Your Own Backyard, A Practical Guide for Growing Vegetables, Fruits, Nuts, Herbs, Medicines and other Useful Products
© 1995 by Martin P. Waterman

Published by:
Loompanics Unlimited
PO Box 1197
Port Townsend, WA 98368

Loompanics Unlimited is a division of Loompanics Enterprises, Inc.
1-360-385-2230
E-mail: loompanx@olympus.net
Web site: www.loompanics.com

ISBN 1-55950-135-9
Library of Congress Card Catalog 95-78038

Contents

To My Grandfather:

You taught me more than you will ever know.

Foreword

The strength of any publication is its writers, and Martin Waterman has been one of the pillars who has made *Backwoods Home Magazine* the dominant how-to, self-reliance magazine in America. I am particularly grateful to him for the high quality gardening articles that continue to attract new readers to the magazine.

In this book dedicated to gardening, he continues to display that thorough knowledge of subject with the same clarity of style I've come to rely upon in the five years of our professional acquaintance.

His approach to conveying information is practical without being boring. No soupy prose here, just hardcore gardening information that is easy to digest, enjoyable to read.

If you're going to read just one gardening book in the '90s, this is the book *Backwoods Home Magazine* will stand behind.

Dave Duffy, Publisher
Backwoods Home Magazine

Introduction

Although this book concentrates on self-sufficiency through the production of food and other commodities, it is by no means limited to simply filling the larder for insurance against uncertain times. There are many additional benefits that can be produced as one becomes more self-sufficient.

For example, self-sufficiency produces freedom. Self-sufficiency puts power in the hands of those who are able to decrease their dependency on others for their own needs. There can be no power without dependency, thus the less you are dependent on others the less power they can exercise over you.

When you produce food, you are producing something of value. Throughout history food and currency have often been one and the same. Even today, when a country's currency collapses, food becomes a currency by default, since it is a commodity necessary to support life.

Even in a stable environment, the food you produce can allow a greater part of your earnings to go to savings; the excess food that you produce can be sold to create income or traded for other goods and services. Self-sufficiency also produces a feeling of pride that you have created something of value and that you can provide for yourself and those around you. There are many other financial, therapeutic and health benefits to growing your own food that are discussed throughout this book.

We live in a time when freedoms are being eroded. Out-of-control government spending and taxes continue to erode our economic freedom. The proliferation of laws has resulted in the fact that each generation has less freedom than the previous one.

The advent of modern technology has not always meant greater freedom and security. In fact, crime statistics continue to worsen, people still go hungry and the number of homeless increases. More and more people are becoming distrustful of government and are seeking ways to put power back in their own hands. The ability to produce food, especially in times of turmoil, has always bestowed power on the producer. In some cases, it has meant the difference between life and death.

I often think of the life of my grandfather. He was born in the late 1800s and died in the 1970s. During his lifetime, he saw turmoil in Europe, two World Wars, the Korean and Vietnam conflicts and the Cold War. To think that we are going to live our lives in a world without upheavals and change may be optimistic, but history has shown us that this type of thinking is not very realistic.

Unfortunately, the practice of being self-sufficient has received a bad name. Those who profit from the *status quo,* and are employed as part of the system, liken the self-sufficiency and survival movements to some kind of radicalism. However, you should keep in mind that this is the same type of radicalism professed by the Founding Fathers of this country, the Bible and progressive and pragmatic thinkers throughout the history of the world.

I became interested in self-sufficiency for very practical and philosophical reasons. I discovered that the practice of growing, nurturing, harvesting and preserving food had many benefits that went far beyond the obvious ones that I had expected. It reinvigorated my spirit and helped me appreciate and focus on some of the more important aspects of existence, while enjoying the abundance that is available for those who wish to take the initiative.

As I began to write on the topic of self-sufficiency through gardening, horticulture, agriculture and other means, I discovered something very reassuring and pleasing: there does exist a large constituency of people who believe that they are better suited to take care of themselves than any government is. Furthermore, many are seeking a lifestyle that is healthier and free of many of the problems and stresses that have become associated with much of our modern-day society. I was surprised to receive letters and phone calls from people who had read my articles seeking to know more about how to start on a road to self-sufficiency. These contacts showed me that there was a need for a book that would bring together concepts and resources needed for anyone looking for greater self sufficiency and security through food production.

Since there are volumes that could be written on the different varieties of food you can grow and preserve, this book will focus first on the theory and then give examples of some of the most efficient and effective methods of growing that can be employed in producing food. Food production and thus the beginning of a more self-sufficient lifestyle is remarkably easy. The nuts and bolts of growing particular foods are readily available and obtainable from gardening books, your local library and from sources listed in the appendix of this book.

This book will give you the steps to help reduce your grocery bill, improve your health through better nutrition, create a long-term supply of emergency food and earn income from your excess production. I have tried to detail the steps so that this can be done in an enjoyable manner at very little or no financial burden or risk to yourself or your family.

When I began to experience the benefits of producing my own food, I began to wish that I had taken the initiative earlier. I had many fears at the beginning but they were all unfounded. If you provide the initiative along with some common sense, the earth, the sun and the rain will be your partners in something that can be a very rewarding and fulfilling enterprise.

Chapter 1

The Basics of Self-Sufficiency Gardening

Probably the most important ingredient for a self-sufficiency gardening plan is assembling adequate information. Research on any project is always time well spent and the practice of small-scale food production is no exception. Taking time to learn as much as possible concerning your future gardening alternatives is one of the most important investments that you can make.

If you were fortunate enough to have grown up on a farm or in a family where gardening was practiced, you will have a definite advantage since this will provide you with a foundation of information, and thus a head start. I started gardening with practically no knowledge of the subject. In retrospect, this was also an advantage since it forced me to study a wide range of options that were available. This, in turn, prompted me to experiment with a wide selection of varieties and methods, some of which I probably never would have otherwise attempted.

If you do come from a gardening family or farming background, try not to be get stuck in a mind-set that may limit the scope of your program. Instead, expand your horizons and try all kinds of new varieties and methods. This has many advantages that will be discussed throughout this book.

Finding Information

Information on gardening and food production is not hard to obtain. Gardening is being touted as the fastest-growing and most popular leisure activity. Just think about how many homes and farms there are in this country and this will give you an idea of the size of the gardening industry. Because of this, it is very easy to obtain the information that you will need.

A garden does not have to occupy much space in order to produce a valuable harvest. (Martin P. Waterman photo.)

Fortunately, one of the advantages of living in the Information Age is that there is so much information available, and this is particularly true with respect to horticulture and agriculture. One added advantage is that much of this information on gardening and related topics can be obtained at little or no charge.

Agriculture is big business, and because of this, Federal, state and even county governments can provide you with ample information to assist you. Much of the information, especially if it is of a local nature, will be applicable to your growing area.

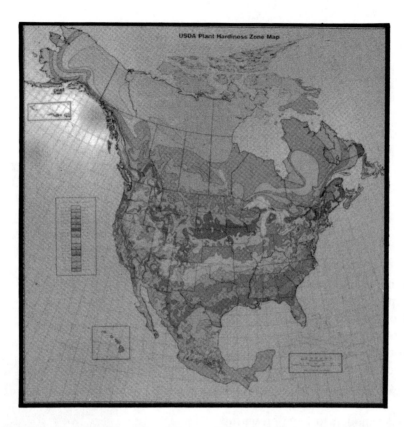

*The U.S.D.A. Plant Hardiness Zone Map can help you understand your climate and
thus the type of plant material that you can successfully grow. (U.S.D.A. photo.)*

Many universities and colleges also have agricultural research programs and because of this, they can be good sources of information. Your library will also have information; it can be a particularly valuable source since it is likely to carry publications that deal with the type of crops that you are considering growing in your area. If your library does not have the gardening information that you require, investigate the inter-library loan service. This is a system whereby librarians can request material from other libraries throughout the country and, in some instances, internationally.

Where Doth Your Garden Grow?

Two of the basic pieces of information that you will need to know is where you are going to grow your food, and the climatic zone you are in. Many plant varieties are rated for certain climatic zones. This rating system is becoming more and more popular, especially with nurseries, garden centers and mail-order firms. Therefore, knowing your zone will

give you an understanding about the types of food plants you can consider growing.

As you become aware of the climatic characteristics of your area, this will naturally shorten the list of plants that you can grow since many will not be able to survive. Knowing your zone can save you money and time and prevent you from growing plant material that has little chance of survival or may not produce a worthwhile yield. For instance, you can forget growing peaches in Zone 3. It is just too cold for them to survive.

You can find the U.S.D.A. hardiness zone map in most gardening books. Even better, you can send $6.50 to the Superintendent of Documents, U.S. Government Printing Office, Washington, D.C., 20402-9325 and you will receive the giant U.S.D.A. hardiness zone map. Once you know the zone in which you are located, you can then select material that will thrive in your area. Most nurseries and seed companies now label their stock so that you will know the zones for which it is suited.

If you grow near the borderline of two zones, be conservative. With so much material available, it would be a shame to have a harsh winter rob you of your valuable fruit trees or other food producing stock. If you are tempted to try material that may be too tender for your zone, limit these choices to 10% or less of your total planting.

Although the hardiness maps and zones are fairly accurate, they do not take into account what are known as microclimates. For instance, you may be in Zone 4, but if you are near a large body of water, or on a south-facing slope, you could actually be in Zone 5 climatically speaking. The water will absorb heat during the day and radiate it back at night, while the southern exposure will absorb more daylight and thus more heat units.

Conversely, if you live in a frost pocket on a north slope, your microclimate could actually be Zone 3. Climatic conditions can change over a few hundred feet of terrain, so it is good to be conservative in your calculations when trying to make a rough estimate of the length of your growing season. You can also obtain information concerning the best varieties for your site from neighbors and local gardening centers or clubs, as well as the numerous gardening publications.

Other excellent sources of material available to help you plan are the numerous free seed and plant catalogs. Most of them have instructions for planting, care and harvesting. Addresses of seed companies can easily be obtained from gardening magazines or from many of the books that I have listed.

Among my best sources of information are the senior citizens and other long-time gardeners in this area. Many of them are familiar with the varieties that have been grown in this area, and some varieties have been successfully grown as long as they can remember. Many of the varieties that they recommend are still the best choices for reliability and production.

Once you know your zone, you can then begin to choose the particular material that you want to grow. The only thing that may change this is that you have a greenhouse, indoor garden or other environment altering circumstances. These aspects will be discussed later in this book. Of course, you could decide to grow certain crops and find that they are not suited for your area. For instance, bananas in northern Florida. One alternative, of course, is to look for that ideal spot for the crops you want to grow even if this means moving to a different area, state or even country.

Many people have migrated to the country or to various specific parts of the country just so they could enjoy the rural lifestyle or take advantage of some of the newer opportunities that can be reaped by small-scale farmers who are able to service lucrative niche markets. If you are considering this type of change in lifestyle, part of your research should be concerned with the types of crops each area will readily support.

If you are living in an apartment or on a small property, you may want to investigate the merits of obtaining a property on which you can produce your own food in some volume. For instance, moving to a home with a larger lot where you can garden may cost an extra $100 per month. However, if you can shave $2,000 off your annual food bill and/or create some income, you could be far ahead financially as well as improving your standard of living.

Start with Growing the Foods You Like

Wherever you may decide to do your growing, especially if you are just starting out, it is best to try starting with some of your favorite foods. For instance, if you like chili or pasta, then you should be testing different varieties of tomatoes, chile peppers, onions, garlic and basil.

By growing the foods that you like, you will find the learning process to be very enjoyable. This is the first step that starts many people on the road to self-sufficiency gardening.

When planning your garden, keep in mind how much time you want to invest in it. One mistake people make is to plant more than they can handle in the beginning and then become overwhelmed or discouraged. Therefore, consider if you want a high-maintenance or low-maintenance planting. Certain vegetables need constant weeding, fertilizing and care to bear a good crop, while others do not. Certain fruit bushes and trees can get by with just some annual or semi-annual pruning. Certain food sources such as nut trees require nearly no maintenance. Any garden that feeds you and your family should contain at least 50% low-maintenance cultivars. This will insure you will still have an acceptable level of food production even if you are not able to devote much time to maintaining it.

There are also many new disease-resistant varieties available for almost any tree, vine or vegetable that you can now grow in order to minimize maintenance. Many seed catalogs offer historic or heirloom seeds. These are the varieties that our grandparents may have grown. They may not be as cosmetically perfect as the newer varieties, but they usually have better taste and, in most cases, have strong disease resistance. Gardening is rarely a static enterprise. I find that my gardening is constantly evolving. For instance, I used to buy tomato plants at the local nursery. However, I soon learned that there were three drawbacks to this. The first was that I was limited to those varieties that the nursery owners chose; second, I had no say about the size, health or quality of the plants; and third, the cost was many times what the cost would be if I started my own plants from seed.

Gardening can be successful whether you are in the frigid north or a tropical or subtropical area.
(U.S.D.A. photo)

One year, I ordered tomato seeds from half-a-dozen seed companies. I tried a dozen new types of tomatoes and from these I found three varieties that performed better than any that were offered for sale in my area. Each year thereafter, I have continued to try 4 or 5 new tomato varieties. I have now settled on about 7 varieties that I will always grow; that is, until a new variety I try is good enough to replace one of the varieties that are among my regulars.

Soil and Fertility

Another consideration in choosing a good gardening site is to be aware of the soil and its fertility. It is very important to try and have the best site possible since this can save you much time and money trying to compensate for missing elements. For instance, some gardeners in Florida are faced with almost pure sand for soil. In order to grow a healthy garden, they have to add a substantial amount of composted and organic material.

The type of soil on a piece of land can change dramatically over a short distance. Your state or local agriculturist should be able to guide you on how to have your soil tested. In some areas the fee is around $5-10. This will tell you your soil pH and then you will know what amendments need to be made, if any. Certain plants need highly acidic soils and therefore your soil may need to be changed, depending on what you plan to grow.

Composting is a skill that every gardener should practice, particularly if you are an organic gardener. *Webster's Dictionary* defines compost as "a mixture of various decaying organic substances, as dead leaves, manure, etc., used for fertilizing land."

Composting adds organic material to the soil and benefits the garden in several ways. Probably the most important advantage of using compost is that the soil structure becomes more porous with better aeration and is then able to retain moisture. The nutrient level of the soil is also improved and less fertilizer becomes needed. A rich, spongy soil produces healthier plants and vegetables by encouraging strong healthy root systems. This makes weeding easier. A rich soil also promotes a healthy earthworm population which is also beneficial for your garden.

If your soil tends to become very hard and compact during dry weather, you probably do not have enough decomposed organic matter or humus as part of your garden soil. If your soil tends to become hard as cement as the gardening season goes on, you definitely should consider adding compost.

The main contributor to organic matter in the soil is the decomposition of the material that remains from your previous year's garden. Unfortunately, this rarely provides enough organic matter, so usually you find that adding various types of organic matter to your soil becomes necessary each year in order to maintain and improve your soil.

Adding compost is relatively easy. It is just a matter of spreading it throughout the garden, and digging or tilling it under. The most common ways are to obtain peat moss or manure and add it to the garden. It is best to use composted manure. If you use fresh manure that has not been allowed to heat up and ferment, the weed seed will not be killed and you run the risk of having many weeds with which to contend. In addition, fresh manure can burn the roots of certain plants.

Make Your Own Compost

Many gardeners opt to make their own compost. Compost bins are available and can be purchased from seed catalogs and garden centers. These bins are used to hold the collected material to be composted such as grass clippings, food scraps and other organic material, in a place where they can start decomposing. With all the concern today about society producing too much garbage, this is a partial solution to the problem because it will not only reduce your garbage and the need for additional landfill areas, but improve your garden as well. It is surprising how many eggshells, fruit and vegetable peelings and other scraps we throw out over the course of a year. It is also a good way to recycle all those garden weeds that you have removed. Some enterprising gardeners purchase leaves from landscapers or sawdust from mills and woodworkers. Some gardeners have found that seaweed works well while others will venture into swamps to gather mosses and other swampy things.

When material is put into a compost pile or bin, it ideally should start heating up; this will start decomposing the material rapidly. Temperatures can reach 140°-160°F, and this high temperature is needed to kill weed seeds, bacteria and plant diseases as well as break down the material so that it is useful in the garden. You can purchase compost thermometers and tools that help to turn and aerate the pile in order to keep the decomposing process going. It is often necessary to add a "starter" to activate or speed up the process. This is usually something containing both nitrogen and protein, such as manure. Good rich garden soil or bone meal will also work well. It is also advisable to make sure the pile is always moist but never too wet or too dry. The pile should be turned every week or so.

If you do not want to purchase a compost bin, one can be quite easily and inexpensively assembled. Many designs have been used, ranging from building large wooden boxes to using turkey or chicken fencing in the shape of a circle. Whatever method you use, your garden will benefit and your vegetables will mature earlier and be of higher quality. Tilling and hoeing are also made much easier and weeds never seem to get a strong hold in loose porous soil.

The Weather Factor

If you are in an area that is prone to drought, you may wish to consider a water irrigation or drip-system. Underground irrigation can save a substantial amount of water, especially in hot and dry climates, since so much water that is applied to the surface will evaporate or not penetrate more than a few inches.

All plants need water but the requirements will vary. If you are growing tomatoes in southern Arizona, you may have to budget more time and money for irrigation than if you were growing them in the Pacific Northwest. Irrigation systems can be designed so that you can leave your plantation for periods of time without worrying about losing plants to drought.

Sunlight is very important for most plants. By planting on a south-facing slope (as opposed to a north-facing one), you can increase the sun exposure your plants will be receiving. However, some plants prefer shade and will do better in cooler temperatures, so a north slope or exposure should be best.

Although this may only result in a few extra moments each day, over the course of a growing season the amount of extra sun and thus the extra crops you can have could be substantial. For some borderline crops, it could make the difference of being able to grow a particular variety in your area.

Starting with foolproof and easy-to-grow varieties will provide a basis for learning while at the same time preventing you from developing reasons to be discouraged. It is always a sound idea to grow a wide range of plants and varieties so that you will always be guaranteed a large harvest.

Make Time Work For You

Another consideration is how much time you will have available to devote to your gardening. Probably one of the most important things you can do is classify your gardening time. For instance, you should think of it as relaxation time; recreation and exercise instead of work. Gardening can be made even more enjoyable in several ways. I like to strap on the Walkman so that I can listen to music as well as informational tapes when I garden. I also find that gardening is most enjoyable if you do it with a friend or companion. If you don't have a gardening friend, place a personal ad. You may be surprised how many people would like to be acquainted with someone who appreciates this popular endeavor.

Guarding the Garden

There is also a question of security. If you are far from your garden, you may be concerned with those who may want to partake of your harvest, whether they are people or critters. Certain areas may need to be fenced. It has been said that good fences make for good neighbors. A fence can serve a number of purposes and one of the most important is that it can conceal your garden as well as protect it from animals and the effects of wind and other environmental damage. It is a great plus if you have neighbors who will keep an eye on your garden if you happen to be away. Security can come in many forms and one of the best is to have a dog. A dog will keep away deer and raccoons as well as other trespassers. Of course, once you start harvesting, the produce can be much more easily protected and stored.

Plant Material

The sources of plant material are almost unlimited and will depend on what you decide to grow. Most people start with local area nurseries and garden centers as their source of material to grow. There are many seed saving and special organizations through which members can trade plant material. These can be a lot of fun and offer a source for material, especially some of the older and more obscure varieties. I personally like the North American Fruit Explorers. They have many members with large collections of historic and new apple, grape and other fruit varieties. It is enjoyable to trade cuttings and seeds with fellow members, many of whom possess a wealth of knowledge which they will share with you. There are many such organizations, and going to their annual conventions or local chapter meetings can be an exciting adventure since it exposes you to a wide variety of produce you can taste. A supermarket carries only a fraction of produce available because most of it is selected for its ability to resist bruising and tolerate long periods of time in transportation and storage. Unfortunately,

flavor and nutrition are usually the trade-off with these supermarket varieties.

Equipment

The best way to handle your equipment needs is to start small. I purchased most of my gardening tools and equipment from yard sales. If you start very small with some container plants and a small patch, you can probably get by with a minimum of hand tools.

When purchasing basic tools such as a hoe and a rake do not purchase the least expensive models or you will be replacing them every year or two. It is best to spend the money and purchase a sturdy well-built tool that will not be awkward for you and hard to use. With your basic equipment it is wise to spend a few extra dollars and invest in a quality product that will last for years or even for decades.

A good garden tiller, new or used, is an investment that will easily pay for itself.
(Martin P. Waterman photo.)

If you are growing a garden of any size, a tiller is a must. A tiller also has another advantage since it is usually very easy to pick up work tilling other people's gardens. You can earn between $20 and $40 per hour doing this. It also creates a customer base should you decide to purchase a small tractor and need some outside income to subsidize its cost until your garden or small farm can really start producing. Tillers can also be rented from equipment rental outlets. Some tillers have the ability to power other machinery such as a chipper or a log splitter. If you are clearing land, these attachments could be very valuable.

Many gardeners expand their growing area to the point where they can support the use of a tractor and other higher-end equipment. You can also use a tractor for cultivating, tilling, creating irrigation ditches, plowing dirt and snow and digging post holes, as well as many other functions. You can also advertise and do work for other people with your tractor.

*Many gardeners have expanded their growing area
so that a small tractor is necessary.*
(Martin P. Waterman photo.)

Horse Power

*Horses and gardening are making a comback
because they are economical, efficient
and enjoyable to work with.*
(Martin P. Waterman photo.)

An interesting note is the number of small farms that are resorting to using horses for farming and gardening. The advantages of using horses are many: firstly, they do not use gas or fuel, which means that in the event of high fuel prices or fuel shortages you have a natural source of horse power; secondly, horses are also one of the best sources of manure, a valuable commodity for growing. You can use it or even sell it.

Horses also do not compact the soil in the same manner as tractors and other equipment. Some tractors require you to place rows four feet apart because of the width between their wheels. Horses allow closer spacing, which means you can plant your rows closer together and plant twice as much per acre. Of course, one of the best benefits of horses is that they are your friends. Remember, horses can even provide you with their offspring. The food you grow will help keep the horses and they will help keep you. Horses are also an excellent means of transportation should you be faced with an emergency where your vehicle is rendered non-operational.

Other Power Alternatives

Consider what would happen if you were suddenly deprived of fuel or electricity. Could you run your basic equipment? Would you lose everything in your refrigerator or your deep freeze? There are many alternative energy systems including solar and wind-powered systems. There are also backup systems such as diesel- or gas-powered electrical generators. There are ample books and magazines available on these types of systems and you should investigate which ones may be best for your needs. These systems can also protect you should there be a large increase in power rates. Of course, there is also the security and peace of mind that occurs when there is one less dependency with which you have to concern yourself.

Getting a Head Start

Other items of equipment to consider are those things that can allow you to start your plants indoors. This can be something very simple such as using ice cream containers or egg and milk cartons. Add some soil and water and put them in a south-facing window (if it is too cold outdoors) and you can produce your own transplants.

Probably the best thing about gardening is that you can start small. Even if you are an apartment dweller, some container tomatoes, cucumbers and other plants, over the course of a season, could give you 50 to 100 pounds of food while you learn the basics and experiment with other cultivars.

Networking

Another thing that can be helpful is to network with other gardeners and growers. Join some of the seed saving or fruit exploring associations. Make new friends that share an interest in the items you are growing and find sources for free plant material (or find those who like to trade). There are many people in the food self-sufficiency movement, although they don't go around announcing it to everyone, for obvious reasons. Having a guaranteed food supply gives them security and allows them the confidence to pursue other aspects of their life.

More and more gardeners are starting to communicate using computers and the Internet and this will be discussed later in the book. I have found that I have always benefited by speaking and interacting with those who share my beliefs and enthusiasm for home food production.

Recommended Reading

Botany for Gardeners: An Introduction and Guide by Brian Capon. Timber Press, Inc., 1990. ISBN 0-88192-258-7. This book is for those who want an easy-to-understand reference book on how plants function, grow and reproduce.

Garden Way's Joy of Gardening by Dick Raymond. Garden Way Inc., 1982. ISBN 0-88266-319-4. One of the best all-around gardening books available. This bestseller has many tips for those gardeners who want extra large harvests.

The Rodale Book of Composting: Easy Methods for Every Gardener edited by Deborah L. Martin and Grace Gershuny. Rodale Press, Inc., 1992. ISBN 0-87857-990-7. This book will show you how to recycle kitchen and yard waste, improve your soil and grow healthier plants.

Successful Small Food Gardens by Louise Riotte. Storey Communications, Inc., 1993. ISBN 0-88266-815-3. This book shows how to get full-size garden yields from very small spaces. An excellent book for both the novice and advanced gardener.

Successful Small Scale Farming: An Organic Approach by Karl Schenke. Storey Communications, Inc., 1991. ISBN 0-88266-642-8. Learn how to plow, manage a woodlot, sell cash crops; it's all in this book.

Chapter Two

Organic Growing

People practice organic gardening for a number of reasons. Personally, I liked the theory of organic gardening because I am fearful of the effects of chemical residues in the food that I eat as well as the food that I prepare and serve to others. When I grow a carrot, apple or a grape, I know exactly what has been applied in order to produce that food. Because I choose to grow my produce organically I can confidently pick grapes fresh from the vine and pop them into my mouth knowing that I am not poisoning my body and damaging my immune system.

For practically any insect there are organic controls and this includes some of the most damaging pests such as fire ants.
(U.S.D.A. photo.)

Another factor to consider, which few people do, is the fact that after applying herbicides, pesticides, fungicides and other chemicals, the residue ends up somewhere. Many farmers can no longer drink the water from their wells since they have now become polluted with the chemicals and fertilizers that have been applied previously to their crops over decades. These same chemicals also run off and find their way into brooks, streams, rivers and lakes, which often renders these bodies of water unfit for supporting life, including that of humans.

It is unfortunate that so many people resist organic gardening principles, especially when they treat them as if they were something new and foreign and to be feared. In actuality, practically everyone gardened or farmed organically until the beginning of this century when chemicals became more widely available and commonplace.

From a survival standpoint, it makes great sense not to garden with chemicals. By breaking the cycle of pesticide, herbicide and fungicide use, you are becoming self-sufficient in your needs for pest controls. In the event of war and other calamities, chemicals may not be available and thus this is another key area where you can break a dependency.

In most instances, there is no need to wage chemical warfare when you want to guarantee a harvest. There are many safer alternatives that can be used to control insects, which can easily replace the use of a favorite chemical. This is especially important when there are children and pets that can be very sensitive in their reaction to the chemicals that are often used.

There are hundreds of techniques that are being used to garden organically. There are also many magazines and books that devote all, or a large part of, their content to the details of growing organically. For any publication, this is quite a brave stance, since it is forgoing a great source of advertising revenue: namely that of the chemical companies.

Some Popular Solutions

There are countless organic solutions, and the following are just a few that have proven to be effective in most instances. As you garden, you will soon learn what works best for your own circumstances.

Many frustrated gardeners want to know how to keep small animals out of the garden without resorting to poisons or traps. It has become politically incorrect, as well as illegal in some areas to kill certain animals; especially if you live in an urban environment. However, there are many solutions to help you get rid of pests without using a scorch-the-earth mentality. For certain small animals, here is a solution that you may wish to try: see if you can locate the entry areas that rabbits and other small animals use to get into the garden. Sprinkle some ground cayenne pepper (or any ground hot pepper) on the path they take. The animals step on the hot pepper. When they lick their paws, they will get a harmless hot tongue. This forces them to remember the garden as an unpleasant place to dine. If this method is successful for you, then you can grow and dry your own hot peppers for this use. Decoys can be effective as well. A plastic owl can keep away certain birds and rodents. It is wise to move it to a different location every few days. There is also the old standby, the scarecrow, which has proven itself effective against both birds and animals.

Again, fences can conceal your garden from both critters and people. Fences can come in many forms. For instance, by surrounding most of your garden with a thicket of blackberries or other thick growing food producing plants, you can limit the entry points to your garden.

There is another way to keep wildlife and other unwanted trespassers out of the garden. It is so simple it should be obvious: a dog! What better way to keep away those nibbling critters! There are some draw-backs, and one is that your dog could go after skunks or porcupines. Before you invest in a dog, do some research about which breeds are best. Certain dogs can be very protective, yet are excellent with small children. If you live in a cold climate, you may not want to have a short-haired dog such as a Doberman Pinscher. Also, it is not humane to leave a dog unattended, since they crave companionship.

Certain animals (and insects) will feed at night during the summer. A simple garden light will deter animals and trick a few insects into thinking that they should stay in their beds and not your garden. For those who have problems with raccoons and other animals, a solution that is often successful is simply placing a radio in a corner of the garden and leaving it on all night. The sound usually scares away raccoons and other animals.

Some gardeners have had success in their fight against pests by placing a plastic dish flush with the soil line. They then fill it with beer. This attracts some harmful grubs and caterpillars that end up drowning (albeit probably happily) in the mixture. Slugs normally take a toll on vegetables such as garden peas. By changing the place where I plant my peas every year, I have had good results. When I plant peas in the same place every year, I usually have a bad infestation. If the outbreak is minor, I don't do anything. If it is a major outbreak, I take the salt shaker and sprinkle salt on the slugs. This kills them quickly. Slugs can also be controlled by simply scattering some lime around the plants upon which they normally feed. Slugs will not cross this lime barrier. If slugs infest your trees, wrap a thin band of copper around the trunk. The slugs will not cross this barrier because copper carries a weak electrical current which the slugs apparently try to avoid.

Chewing tobacco is an age old remedy which has also proven to be effective. It is placed in small piles throughout the garden. Many insects are attracted to it because of its sweetness. They feed on the tobacco which kills them rapidly. This is great because it spares them the pain of nicotine addiction! Ashes from a wood stove can also be an effective control. I often take a can and punch many holes in the bottom of it with a nail. I fill it with ashes and sprinkle cabbage, broccoli and potato plants. I find that in most cases this method controls a number of damaging insects.

Garden cleanliness is a good preventive step for pest control. By gathering fruit that has fallen, piles of garden cuttings and other material, you can eliminate the hiding and overwintering places that are home to many damaging insects.

On the preventive side, you should always check to see if there are plant varieties available to you that are resistant to the diseases found in your area. Many vegetables and fruit varieties are bred to be resistant to a number of diseases and other problems.

An ancient practice which is also recommended in the Bible is giving the garden a rest or rotating the place where you plant your garden. This will eliminate or alleviate insect and disease problems. Certain insects and pests will not travel very far, especially if they are the kind of insects that live in the soil. Thus, a new planting location can be very beneficial for keeping the pest population under control.

Another practical and easy way to administer a solution is the practice of growing a wide variety of vegetables, flowers and plants. By doing this, you set up a "miniecosystem" which will not only encourage a variety of insects but a variety of *predator* insects which will feed upon the insects that you want to eliminate. This creates a balance. When the population of damaging insects increases, so does the predator population.

If you continually have a problem with certain vegetables or other garden varieties, the insects may be too entrenched to be eradicated. By not growing the vegetable for a while, you could have the best solution to the problem because the insects will move on to other areas. With so many crops from which to choose, there really is no need to grow some of the most disease- and pest-prone plants, especially if you plan on gardening organically.

Live animal traps can be used to safely capture small animals such as rabbits and squirrels. This should only be done as a last resort. Try not to trap small animals in the spring because you may be separating mothers from their young who need them for food and protection. The captured animals can then be taken on a picnic or a trip where they can be released into the wild. Remember to check the cages daily and to handle all creatures with care. Also, never use tuna as a bait because it will attract cats. Marshmallows work best for raccoons.

Garden netting can also be useful. It can be moved around the garden as needed. For instance, it can cover strawberries, then cherries and then other crops as they ripen. The netting can help to keep away certain birds. However, one has to be mindful so that birds do not get tangled up in the nets. Some jurisdictions have harsh and ridiculous laws and penalties for killing song birds.

If you have some unanswered questions on how to organically control certain pests, talk to older gardeners or senior citizens. They were gardening before most chemicals came into use and may be able to provide you with safer solutions. In fact, many of the solutions in this chapter were learned from older gardeners. It is also advisable to see what your neighbors and those in your area may be using; then you can learn from their mistakes and duplicate their successes.

Of course, if you need more information, don't forget to use your library and your local Department of Agriculture (make your tax money work for you) to find out about pest control alternatives. Also, ask local garden center personnel to learn what your alternatives are before using any pest programs. Most sprays do not discriminate between harmful and beneficial insects. After spraying, the harmful ones usually rebound in greater numbers than the beneficial insects because the harmful insects usually have shorter life cycles. Before the population of the beneficial insects (that naturally feed on the harmful ones) rebounds, you may have to spray again. Thus, you can find yourself hostage to a spray program resulting in bigger infestations every time you spray. So remember, sometimes the solution is worse than the problem.

Although it is not the case with every variety, heirloom and historic seeds often are more pest- and disease-resistant. Many of the seeds our forefathers (and -mothers) used were closer to the wild form. They may not have the same crisp, photogenic supermarket appearance, but many excel in flavor and disease resistance. Most seed catalogs contain several varieties which are usually listed as historic or heirloom varieties.

Some flying insects cannot easily be detected until they have done their damage. Certain types of traps are available that work on a number of different principles. Some use color, such as the apple maggot trap which is usually a red croquet ball covered with a sticky substance such as Tangletrap. By hanging this trap on an apple tree, you will attract the apple maggot fly. The female fly will think the trap is a big juicy apple and an ideal place to lay her eggs, not being able to recognize it for the sticky situation it really is.

Other traps use sexual attractants, which are chemicals that imitate the sexual attractant of the female of the species that you want to control. The male insects are attracted and killed. The females then do not produce offspring. These traps are usually called "pheromone traps," and are commonly available for a number of different moths, maggots and worms. Check with your local nursery or state Agriculture Department. Both can usually suggest what is best for your area.

This U.S.D.A. scientist has just attached a pheromone strip to an apple tree branch. The pheromones will disrupt the mating of destructive insects and thus minimize the damage.
(U.S.D.A. photo.)

There are many homemade mixtures that will not harm humans but are toxic to certain insects. Using dishwater or dishwashing liquid (diluted 40 to 1 with water) can be a good way to control the outbreaks of aphids and some other types of insects. The solution breaks down fairly easily, does not harm most plants and usually kills the bugs before they realize that they are soaking in it. According to the U.S.D.A., there is a new safe and effective home pesticide that has been developed by scientists at the Agricultural Research Service. It is available to everyone. It is the same dishwashing liquid mixture but with a simple added ingredient. The scientists found that by adding some cooking oil to the concoction, it becomes even more effective and toxic to insects. For humans, it is safe, nontoxic, simple to prepare and costs only pennies per application. To make the mixture, you take one

cup of oil (peanut, safflower, soybean, corn, sunflower, etc.) and add one teaspoon of detergent. This is your base concentrate mixture. When needed, take one or two teaspoons of the concentrate and add it to one cup of water and then spray it on your plants.

Cornell University in New York reports that sodium bicarbonate (yes, baking soda) will act as a fungicide which is effective against powdery mildew and black spot. The best combination tested so far (and only on roses with black spot) was a mixture of .5% baking soda and water (200 parts water to 1 part baking soda). Researchers still do not understand how or why this mixture works.

Many plants will also deter certain pests. Many organic gardeners have known for some time that garlic is a natural pest deterrent when grown in the garden. It can also be used to make an effective mixture by putting a few garlic cloves in a blender with some water and then pressing the blend button. The mixture is then sprayed on your plants which are being eaten by the pests. There is currently research being conducted to find out more about how garlic can deter pests.

Another simple way to rid yourself of insects is to use your hands. Potato bugs can be gathered and their eggs squashed. Caterpillars can be squashed, but you may want to wear gloves if you are squeamish. I usually squeeze the leaves that have leaf rollers in them to crush them. They are easily crushed this way.

The Colorado Potato Bug causes substantial damage to many crops. Historically it has been controlled with harsh chemicals but more and more it is now being controlled with organic methods.
(U.S.D.A. Photo.)

Many of the commercial strawberry farmers in California have adopted a new way to control pests. Rather than applying chemicals to eradicate insect pests as they did in the past, they now have a new machine that they use. As it passes over the strawberry rows, the machine vacuums up the pests from the plants. This may have been the inspiration behind some other techniques about which I have been hearing. Gardeners are now gathering potato bugs with a vacuum cleaner or a dust buster.

Of course, there are also pests such as deer and other large animals. Many farmers have had problems with deer nibbling on more than their fair share of the crops. Two solutions seem to work well. The first is to put pails of human urine at the corners of the field. The second is more recent and definitely more civil. This method involves hanging bars of soap in different spots around your property. It is believed that deer have learned to recognize hunters by the smell of soap. One California farmer, after testing, finds Dial soap works best. It may be a good idea to ask the hunters in your area about the type of soap they usually use.

One of the best cures for certain insect infestations is the use of chickens. Many orchard owners have found that not only will the chickens find and eat many of the insects, including insect larvae on the ground, but they will also turn the insects into valuable manure for the soil. Some organic plum farmers go through their orchards and shake the trees, which causes the plum curculios to roll up into balls and fall to the ground, where the chickens soon gobble them up.

Lady Bugs are a beneficial insect and should be encouraged. You can even order them through the mail.
(Martin P. Waterman photo.)

If you lack predatory insects in your garden, there is a solution. You can order by mail from companies that specialize in predatory insects. Check the advertisements in the back of organic gardening magazines to find out more about these mail-order predatory bugs. Some of the varieties available are predatory wasps, lady bugs and the praying mantis. Spiders can eat their share of damaging bugs. Even though they like branches, one of their favorite structures on which to build webs is a wooden trellis or arbor where their webs can be secure. Certain plants such as marigolds, dill and spearmint are known to attract spiders.

If you really want to get rid of a large population of harmful insects, you should learn to like non-poisonous snakes. If you have any small boys, they will love you for it. A garter snake will eat all kinds of insects and lots of them. King snakes will eat gophers, and many species of non-poisonous snakes will eat mice and rats. Another benefit is that snakes will also frighten off many species of birds which like to land and feed on your garden.

Many gardeners encourage reptiles and amphibians to move into their gardens by providing them with hiding places and water. These creatures reward the gardener by continually cleaning harmful pests out of the garden. Toads are a good example of a beneficial amphibian that will eat four times their stomach's capacity in a twenty-four hour period. A habitat for toads can be created by using an overturned clay pot with an entrance chipped into it. The pot can be partially buried in soil to keep the toad home cool. Toad homes can also be built out of stone.

Bats are useful to organic gardeners. A single bat can devour thousands of insects each night, including many which can be detrimental to your garden. Bat houses can be built to give these beneficial winged wonders a resting place during the day. For more information on bat houses, write Bat Conservation International, P.O. Box 162603, Austin, Texas, 78716. Also, many seed companies which sell bird houses are now selling bat houses. Bats have developed a bad reputation which is undeserved, because they play a beneficial role as an integral part of the ecosystem.

One of the most neglected forms of pest control is simple tilling of the soil, especially before the start of the season and at the end of it. The tilling will expose insect eggs and larvae to the weather as well as to predators. One of the drawbacks is that the tiller's blades do not discriminate, and beneficial insects are often unfortunately killed.

If you have a small area with an endless number of pests, you may want to try pasteurizing your soil. To do this, you need to procure some large plastic sheets from a building supply store. This is the clear plastic that is used in home construction to form vapor barriers, and 3 mil. is thick enough for this purpose. When the plastic is spread out and anchored over an area of soil, the resulting heat from the sun is such that it will kill insects, larvae and eggs in the soil.

As you garden, you will learn certain tricks for cultivating healthier and hardier plants. I have found that waiting longer than usual in the spring to put transplants in the garden will make them more resistant to insect and disease problems. The extra time allows the plants to grow and become more mature. Doing this apparently makes them better prepared for the stresses of life in the garden. In my experience, I have found that this delay in planting is particularly helpful as far as tomatoes, peppers and cabbage are concerned.

Much damage seems to occur around transplanting time. If cutworms topple your young transplants, then consider this simple solution: take a cardboard milk carton and remove the top and bottom. Cut the remaining square tube into one-inch strips. Place these around your young transplants. You will find that cutworms are unable to get through the cardboard and chop down your young transplants.

If you must grow certain crops and cannot organically defeat insects with sprays or other deterrents, you can use plastic screendoor mesh to save some of your crops. This mesh is available in rolls and sold by the foot at many hardware and building supply stores. The mesh can be cut into squares of differing sizes which can be held in place with clothes pins. Try this mesh around vines to prevent birds from eating grapes and other berries. The same method can be used with corn to prevent feasting by grasshoppers and other insects. In addition, mesh can be used to protect other fruit and vegetable crops. Although this method can be time-consuming, having some crop to harvest is better than having no crop.

We are learning much more about organic gardening as it becomes more popular. Usually, most of it has been practiced for thousands of years. For example, researchers at Cornell University have found that collards which were fertilized with manures were less prone to insect damage than those fertilized with chemical fertilizers. Scientists are not sure why this is so, but they did note that more birds frequented the collards that were fed manure.

Mulching has also been shown to have benefits besides the simple addition of organic matter to the soil and retention of moisture. Some plants such as potatoes can thereby be protected from the Colorado potato beetle. It is thought that the mulch provides a big obstacle for the beetles and hinders them from being able to seek out the potato plants.

These are but a few solutions that I have found that work for me. I am continually learning new techniques all the time, and since the organic gardening movement is growing, the future for new products, varieties and techniques looks particularly bright.

I do not purchase herbicides, pesticides or fungicides. This saves me money and also saves me the anxiety and worry that I may be slowly poisoning myself, those close to me and the soil. Even with chemical controls, you will always lose part of your crops in certain years to pests and diseases. Many chemicals are rendered ineffective if applied at the wrong time or in the wrong concentrations. Excessive sun or rain can also render many chemicals useless.

Organic gardening is a philosophy based on the belief that the health of yourself, your family and the planet takes precedence over using often dangerous practices in order to possibly guarantee a larger and less-blemished harvest. You accept the facts that all organisms have their place in Mother Nature, and that it is acceptable at times to lose part of your harvest to a fellow and vital part of the ecosystem. Once you accept that working with, instead of against, Mother Nature is consistent with your objectives for survival, you can make the necessary adjustments and get on with your worry-free gardening.

Recommended Reading

Rodale's Garden Problem Solver: Vegetables, Fruits and Herbs by Jeff Ball. Rodale Press Inc., 1988. ISBN 0-87857-762-9. This book is an excellent resource on how to solve over 700 garden problems, and consistent with other Rodale books, it offers safe alternatives to harsh chemicals and drastic treatment methods.

The Organic Gardener's Handbook of Natural Insect and Disease Control: A Complete Problem-Solving Guide to Keeping Your Garden & Yard Healthy without Chemicals edited by Barbara Ellis and Fern Marshall Bradley. Rodale Press, Inc., 1992. ISBN 0-87596-124-X. More than 350 photographs to help you identify beneficial and harmful insects, plus an organic problem-solving encyclopedia covering more than 200 vegetables, fruits, herbs, flowers, trees and shrubs.

Shepherds Purse: Organic Pest Control Handbook for Home and Garden. The Book Publishing Company, 1992. ISBN 0-913990-98-1. A short and concise book that features an excellent reference section on where to purchase beneficial insects and organic pest control supplies.

Step By Step Organic Vegetable Gardening: The Gardening Classic Revised and Updated by Shepherd Ogden. HarperCollins Publishers, 1992. ISBN 0-06-016668-1. A classic indeed, this book is considered an organic gardening Bible by many growers.

Common-Sense Pest Control: Least-toxic Solutions for Your Home, Garden, Pets and Community by William Olkowski, Sheila Daar, and Helga Olkowski. The Taunton Press, Inc., 1991. ISBN 0-942391-63-2. This book contains 736 pages of valuable information on controlling a wide spectrum of pests.

Fences for Pasture & Garden by Gail Damerow. Storey Communications, Inc., 1992. ISBN 0-88266-753-X. How to keep wildlife out of your garden and keep your own livestock inside, plus information on trellises and gates.

Chapter Three

Vegetable Growing

Growing vegetables is only intimidating for the uninitiated and the unenlightened. Once people start growing their own food, they are often surprised to find how simple and natural the process can be.

Since many of our cultivated crops are only a few generations removed from their wild ancestors, and these plants have survived millenniums without the benefit of being tended, irrigated, fertilized or weeded, certain vegetable varieties can actually tolerate a degree of neglect.

A small vegetable patch does not need a tremendous amount of care or investment. However, as your patch grows bigger, the few seconds it may take to pull some weeds around each plant can quickly multiply if you are growing a thousand of them. The key is to not grow so much that your garden is beyond the realm of what you are able to, or want to maintain.

I must confess that I, at first, was very intimidated by the growing process, and this was because I did not understand it. I grew up in a large city, and the concept of growing plants was foreign to my way of thinking. At that time, my perception was that farming was a very difficult and complex practice. After all, it seemed to be commonplace to hear news reports of farmers in trouble, so naturally I assumed that farmers were, perhaps, engaged in a never ending losing battle against the weather, Mother Nature, low prices, diseases, pests and ill-conceived and regressive government policies and bankers.

I have a great respect for farmers, but unfortunately, many of them are destined to fail. Many are trapped in the cycle of growing commodity crops which are continually being undermined by various foreign governments who pay their farmers many times the world price in order to support farms which are not even viable in today's economy. Since the farmers are a political force in many countries, they can continue their inefficient practices and undermine world prices. One of the benefits of self-sufficiency gardening is that the number-one person you are trying to satisfy is yourself. Any excess produce can be marketed in your area, a domain which is easily served and understood by you. You usually do not need any permits, and the marketplace, not a marketing board, will be telling you the prices you can charge for your products.

Growing Vegetables vs. Buying

There are many instances in which you should be purchasing vegetables instead of growing them. Let me explain. In my area there are many potato farmers. In the autumn, I can purchase a 50-pound bag of Number 2 potatoes for $2.97. That is less than six cents per pound. I cannot grow them that inexpensively, since, of course, I am not subsidized or paid by the government to grow them. Also, my growing space is at a premium, and why should I grow something that sells for six cents per pound when I could grow something with a greater yield and less need for chemical controls that sells for 60 cents per pound?

I have found, in this particular area, that it is cheaper for me to buy certain vegetables such as potatoes, corn and other produce than it is to grow it. You will probably run into a similar situation in your area. For instance, if you are surrounded by cabbage farms, you would be better off to purchase or trade for cabbage and focus on a higher value crop.

Instead of growing a crop such as potatoes, I usually find that I am better off growing something like tomatoes. It is rare in this area to ever see fresh tomatoes, even in season, sell for under ninety-nine cents per pound.

To every rule there are exceptions. I will often plant some early maturing potatoes in order to grow a supply of fresh potatoes early in the season. At this time, potatoes are usually selling at a premium and can command prices of between twenty and thirty cents per pound. In addition, fresh potatoes are truly a gourmet item, especially if you grow a selection of some of the lesser known and historic varieties that have a more pronounced flavor than the majority of the neutral flavored commercial cultivars.

In the debate about whether to purchase or grow certain vegetables and other varieties, there is something that even the best writer in the world cannot properly convey. That is the taste, the smell, and the appearance of fresh produce from the garden. It is a standard for which the best restaurants strive, and they charge their patrons fortunes for fresh morsels of locally grown produce. You, too, can have access to the highest quality, most nutritious and freshest produce available, and the benefits from this go far beyond the security aspects. It is also an important factor to consider when choosing the type of food you wish to grow.

Once you are growing produce or creating value-added preserves or food, you will have something to trade with other growers in order to expand the foods that are available for your use. Growers will regularly trade produce since most will tend to specialize in certain items. It is best to make arrangements before the start of the season. You may be surprised how easy it is to find someone who wants the produce you are growing and will also have something that you want.

Of course, one of the most important benefits of fresh produce is that the food has its highest nutritional value when fresh. A big part of surviving in this ever changing world is a healthy body and mind, and good nutrition is the fuel our body needs to function at its optimum level. Many people in the self-sufficiency movement often take this part of the equation for granted, relying instead on various forms of hardware which are no substitute. You may be armed to the teeth, but remember: you can't eat bullets.

Growing crops that will produce a bumper harvest is usually not a problem. Instead, the difficulty usually lies in not taking the time to establish a market for your produce. However, for the small growers, this is no problem, since they can grow and preserve what they want. This also provides them with a stable base for expansion should they begin to sell some of their harvests.

One last item about buying vegetables or any other produce: never buy retail if you can avoid it. If you want 100 pounds of peanuts or onions, find a wholesale food broker and simply tell them you are a caterer. This is usually what I do, and there is nothing misleading about this statement since I cater to my own selfish desires to save money and be self-sufficient. You may be refused by some brokers, but somebody will eventually sell to you. You can also purchase a few hundred pounds of rice and similar foods that you will probably never be able to grow economically. Of course, with all your fresh vegetables and produce, there is nothing wrong with doing some catering. People are always having weddings, birthdays and other celebrations, and as you become more involved in the production and preparation of food, this could be another natural outlet through which to create added income and thus extra security.

Another method which helps in purchasing wholesale is getting some of your friends to pitch in on a big order. Also be aware that the possibility exists that you can take some of the wholesale food you purchase and resell it for a profit. I know of many growers who sell at farmers' markets who will head to a produce wholesaler the moment they run out of vegetables. They may not be making as much money, but they are still making enough profit to justify their presence.

Short-Term, Mid-Term and Long-Term Needs

For self-sufficiency gardening, there are three immediate needs you should consider when planting your vegetable garden. They are the short-term, the mid-term and the future. Let me explain. There are certain foods which can be grown quite quickly. Bean sprouts and alfalfa sprouts can be ready in days; lettuce in less than a month. This type of strategy can provide food in a relatively short period of time. It is always a good practice to be prepared with enough seed so that you can be into food production very quickly.

Even if there are no emergencies, when you are producing a large portion of vegetables and food that you would normally have to pay for on your grocery bill, this mo... ...l for other areas of your ...asing your security. Even ...roduce several thousand ...son.

...ort-term food supply in ...good supply of seeds ...em in the order of the ...iability over time. Select ...t be afraid to try new ...ery quick crops, lettuce ...omenal array of habits, ...s.

...getables that can take ...satisfy the mid-term ...this might be tomatoes ...rm requirements might ...which require a longer ...ill fit into a number of ...can be ready for fresh ...ey can also be dried, ...your long-range food

...ular ...rieties

...gin in self-sufficiency ...nall patch containing ...arden varieties. The ...r a reason. They are ...vell as being versatile ...offer many storage

...ver the definition of ...etable. Scientifically, ...l use the accepted ...ses of this book.

...rop that traces its ...s a long history of ...as been found in the

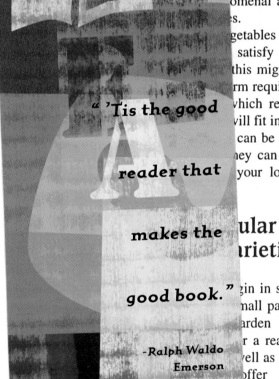

form of paintings on Egyptian tombs that are over 5,000 years old.

Asparagus is a very early crop and is a perennial, which means that once planted, and if properly maintained, your asparagus will come up year after year. Asparagus is a good cash crop and it seems to be desirable in practically any market. It almost always commands a good price.

It takes several years for an asparagus bed to come into full production, so this is the reason many people do not bother growing it. Fresh asparagus does not keep very well and is prone to drying out. Asparagus can be canned, dried and stored in many different ways, however. It is also considered a gourmet vegetable.

It is wise to look into other perennial vegetable crops such as rhubarb, Jerusalem artichokes, horse-radish and many new foreign and exotic crops that are becoming available. It is a good idea to structure your garden so that a large percentage of the plants you grow are perennial crops which will sprout regularly year after year.

Beans

There are many different types of beans. These include soybeans, shell beans, dry beans and snap beans. From a self-sufficiency standpoint, dry beans are one of the best crops that can be grown since they can be stored for decades and offer an excellent source of protein. Furthermore, dried beans can be used in soups, stews, and, of course, traditional dishes such as chili and baked beans. Beans can also be included in many recipes and can be preserved using a variety of methods.

Derby Bean is an All-America Selection winner owing to its superior flavor and reliability.
(All-America Selections photo.)

I like growing a multipurpose bean such as French Horticultural. When young, the whole pod can be boiled or pickled; when mature, the beans can be dried for storage or cooked. I also like red kidney beans, which can are great in bean salads or soups. Fresh beans can be a relatively early crop, with some being ready to harvest in as little as seven weeks. They are sensitive to frosts, so you must wait until soil and air temperatures are sufficiently warm. Another advantage to beans is that several varieties will grow in soil that is too poor to support other crops.

Beets

Beets are one of the best storage vegetables. They will also provide you with a quick source of healthy and tasty greens early in the season when fresh vegetables may be scarce. In many places in Europe as well as in other countries and regions, beets are considered a delicacy.

Beets come in a number of colors other than the most familiar red varieties, and these are quickly being adopted by restaurants. Some varieties of beets have a high sugar content, and beets eventually were bred to have as much sugar as sugar cane.

Beets are nutritious and can be used in many recipes. They can also be prepared so that they can be stored for long periods of time.
(Photo by Martin P. Waterman.)

I have no problem having beets year-round. Early in the season I eat beet greens, followed by young baby beets that are harvested as I thin the rows. In the fall I have plenty of beets for canning or storage. They are versatile in the kitchen, and many gourmet recipes (I am partial to beets with orange sauce) employ this healthy vegetable. One pound of beets has only 78 calories. Some varieties are ready to harvest in about eight weeks. Beets are related to spinach and chard, which are also excellent sources of fast growing and nutritious greens.

Broccoli, Brussels Sprouts, Cabbage & Cauliflower

Recently these vegetables have been in the news because of their ability to strengthen the body's immune system, as well as the documented studies that show they can help in the prevention of certain types of cancer. These are all members of the genus *brassica,* which also includes kale, kohlrabi and a number of Chinese cabbages such as pak-choi and pe-tsai.

All these vegetables are relatively easy to grow, and because of this can often be purchased quite inexpensively during the growing season.

Broccoli is versatile and can be used in a number of recipes including salads, stir-frys and soups.

Brussels sprouts are actually very small cabbages which grow in along the stem and sprout at the leaf axis. They originated in Belgium and can sell for a premium price in many markets, especially during the winter months. I particularly like to freeze at least 50 pounds of these nutritious vegetables.

Cabbage comes in many different varieties such as red, savoy and white, and making a selection can be difficult. Some of the older varieties can produce heads which can be quite large. These were more popular in the olden days when people had larger families. One variety, Hercules, holds the world's record weighing in at 124 pounds.

Cauliflower now comes in several colors other than the familiar white varieties. There is even a hybrid of cauliflower crossed with broccoli which has become very popular in some areas. Cauliflower can be dried, but one of the most popular ways to store this healthy variety is to pickle it.

Carrots

Carrots do not often get the respect that they deserve. Large harvests are easy to achieve, and *Daucus carota* can subsequently be dried for use later in soup or stew mixtures. Carrots will also keep in a root cellar or cool area for long periods of time if properly prepared. There are many varieties available, and I always choose a few of the best storage types. Some carrots, especially some of the older historic varieties that were also used for cattle feed, can get quite large. Some of the baby carrots are popular offerings at restaurants and grocery stores, as the smaller bunches of gourmet carrots are desirable to seniors and single people who are looking for smaller serving sizes.

Corn

Corn is a fantastic food to grow because it can be stored in so many different ways. Often it is cheaper to purchase corn than to grow it, so your precious gardening space may be better utilized by growing a crop that is of greater value.

Growing your own grains can allow you to make your own breads and pastas. Self-sufficiency should not result in boring foods.
(U.S.D.A. photo.)

One form of corn that is easy to store is popcorn, but chances are that you can probably purchase the kernels in bulk much cheaper than you can grow them.

Some gardeners choose to grow corn which is dried and made into their own organically produced corn flour. This, in turn, can be used to make corn breads, tortillas and many other foods. I always like to grow some of the super sweet varieties for fresh eating during the season, and sometimes some for freezing and canning.

Garlic

Garlic is one of my favorite crops. Firstly, I find I can never grow enough of this crop, and no matter how much I grow, I never have trouble selling or trading it. Secondly, garlic does wonderful things to salads, sauces, chilis and other recipes. Garlic is also known to deter certain insects and pests from munching in your garden. If you have spent any time in the kitchen, you will know how important garlic can be. In my climate, I plant the cloves in the autumn and they are ready to harvest in the late summer. I also use the greens and young garlic in much the way I employ small onions.

As if this were not enough, garlic is one of the healthiest foods that you can grow, and has received much attention from the press for its curative powers. Healthful foods such as garlic have great potential, because as the population ages, healthful foods are becoming better known and in greater demand.

Lettuce

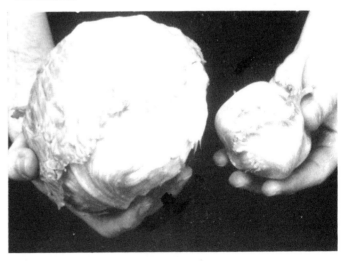

Lettuce is fast growing and nutritious. On the right is a newly developed mini-lettuce compared to a standard sized head of lettuce.
(U.S.D.A. photo.)

Lettuce is truly an amazing crop. You can sow the seeds and have edible leaves in a very short time; often mere weeks. My first salads of the year are a result of thinning the salad plants about ten days to two weeks after they have emerged. Because most lettuces prefer cooler temperatures, it can be started early or in a cold frame or unheated greenhouse. One of the nice things about lettuce is that because it is so fast-growing, you can start harvesting leaves within a short time of planting.

The best way to grow lettuce is to continually stagger your plantings so that you can have a fresh supply throughout the season. In addition to being tasty, lettuce has great nutritional value. Most lettuce does not grow well in hot weather, so I grow most of mine early or late in the season.

Most people are only familiar with iceberg and romaine lettuce. There are many other types and some of them are much more tasty than the rather bland supermarket varieties. I try to grow a wide selection of lettuces, since fresh lettuce is a treat indeed. Many seed companies such as Thompson & Morgan sell seed packets with mixed varieties.

Melons

Melons can offer possibilities for the fresh market. If you are in an area where you can grow melons, there usually exist opportunities to sell your produce. Most melons do not keep well, but they are always in demand if you are able to keep your prices competitive.

Onions

I once had a chef tell me that the onion is, without a doubt, the most important and most versatile food used in cooking. At the time this seemed like a strange statement, but over the years I have found that he was totally accurate.

Of course, one of the advantages of growing your own onions is that you are not limited to the rather lackluster selection at your local supermarket. There are many different varieties of onions, and thus you can probably find a niche to fill by growing something different.

It is almost impossible to make mistakes growing onions. If you keep them weeded, watered and well-nourished, the yields can be staggering.

Peas

Few gardeners are aware that there are numerous types of peas which can be grown. Since many of

them can be dried, they are ideal for long-term storage. Some varieties of peas can be sown early in the spring while there are still frosts and the soil is wet and damp. This can provide a very early harvest of peas. I find that fresh peas are like candy. I eat them continually during the season and use them in salads and other recipes. I will also freeze and dry peas.

Case Study — Peppers

They are, in fact and in practice, the number-one spice ingredient in the world. Most people think that there are only two types of sweet peppers: red or green. But more often than not, green bell peppers are red peppers which were picked before they ripened. There are also many varieties of hot peppers just waiting to be exploited.

Peppers are ideal plants for the self-sufficiency gardener, and are underutilized. This is because most growers are acquainted with very few varieties and their uses.

Even though thousands of varieties of peppers are available, seed companies must limit their selection of pepper varieties to just a few. As a result, most gardeners are not exposed to the broad spectrum of varieties unless they deal with one of the seed houses that specialize in pepper varieties. Add to this the fact that growers, large and small, tend to choose common commercial varieties that will have mass appeal, and you begin to see why this common and recognizable vegetable has not been fully explored. Peppers are one crop, because of the wide selection, that offers opportunities to growers to provide the restaurant, roadside market and grocery trade with something that is familiar, yet new and exciting.

In case you have not noticed, peppers are becoming more and more popular. Hot peppers definitely have the edge in the popularity contest. Hot peppers have even spawned legions of devoted fans that aptly call themselves "Chile-Heads." And the rising fame of the pepper is not limited to being a North American phenomenon. Peppers are also responsible for turning often bland European cuisine into exciting new meals. Traditional fare everywhere is now being presented in hotter versions. This is consistent with the changing attitudes and times, as the popularity of ethnic foods and hotter foods is on the rise.

Of course, without peppers, certain dishes would not be possible. Imagine trying to eat chili, salsa,

Cajun, Creole, Mexican, East Indian or Szechwan food without hot peppers. It would render these foods unrecognizable.

Hot peppers are continuing to ignite meals and taste buds and threaten to do much more for North American cuisine than tomatoes did for Italian.

Super Cayenne is a very productive hot pepper that has proven its reliability.
(All-America Selections photo.)

Sweet peppers are also gaining in popularity, because they are a low-calorie food packed with vitamins and nutrition. As our population of baby boomers ages, more attention is given to preventive medicine, diet and light cuisine. This has made sweet or bell peppers more popular in everything from salads to vegetarian pizzas. Because of its versatility, it is hard to conceive that at one time all peppers were obscure and rarely found in gardens, restaurants or supermarkets.

Cultivation

Many people feel that growing peppers is too difficult, since they can often be finicky. Many gardeners take the attitude that there is little reason to grow something that is so readily available year-round at the supermarket. True, peppers can be finicky and do succumb to many diseases and climatic pressures. Once you understand their requirements, however, you will be more than halfway home. The other part of the equation usually consists of choosing the correct varieties for your specific environment. Whether you are new to growing peppers or a veteran *peppermeister,* one of the most important things you can do to guarantee success is to try cultivating a wide variety yourself, as well as determining which varieties do well for fellow gardeners and growers in your area. Remember that some peppers have diverse bloodlines, and their requirements can vary.

Peppers should be started indoors about six to eight weeks before transplanting. They do very well under fluorescent lights, and they do not become leggy like their relative the tomato. The seeds take from 8-20 days to germinate and will do best if the soil is warm, between 65°F and 85°F.

Peppers are, for the most part, a subtropical and warm weather vegetable. They are very tender and will not tolerate any frost. Peppers, as a general rule, seem to grow best when soil temperatures exceed 60°F. Air temperatures during the day are between 65°F to 85°F and during the night between 60°F to 75°F. Peppers are usually planted 12-14 inches apart.

Peppers require full sun and do not do well in shaded areas. In the north, covering peppers early in the season in plastic tunnels can help in accelerating growth and guaranteeing a crop. Peppers also do very well in a greenhouse environment, and this is an ideal way to extend your season for extra early and late crops. According to Thompson & Morgan, who provide seeds for cooler climates such as those which exist in Britain, "Hot peppers need high temperatures whilst the fruit are developing. The higher the temperature the hotter the pepper, best grown in the greenhouse, conservatory or windowsill."

Generally speaking, peppers require about an inch of water per week. This is particularly important from flowering time through the harvest. Peppers also like a rich soil with a pH range between 6.0 and 7.0. Slow-acting fertilizers seem to be best, and peppers will also benefit from light feedings, applied as side dressings or foliar sprays, on a monthly basis. It is especially important to make sure the peppers are fed within a few weeks after transplanting, and after the first fruit has begun to set.

One of the most common pepper problems is the failure to set fruit. The causes for this are usually cool weather or transplanting varieties before the warm weather has arrived. For cooler climates, variety selection becomes a must.

If your pepper plant produces narrow greenish-yellow leaves, this is usually an indicator of phosphorus deficiency which is likely to occur in acid soils. This can be remedied by fertilizer applications or the use of wood ashes.

Too much fertilizer can lead to too much vegetative growth with an absence of fruit. In some soils, it may be wiser to only fertilize after the fruit has been set. Overfeeding is one of the most prevalent mistakes people make with peppers.

As far as pests are concerned, peppers are vulnerable to aphids, cutworms, European corn borers, flea beetles, leaf miners, mites, nematodes, tomato hornworms and weevils. Diseases that are common are anthracnose, bacterial spot, blossom-end rot and tobacco mosaic. The first line of defense against any pest or disease is to produce healthy plants by making sure they get all the items that they require for healthy growth. Many pests can be eliminated by practicing companion planting and growing resistant varieties. There are many texts on organic solutions, and this approach combined with other practices can help guarantee a healthy harvest.

Keeping the Harvest

The exact time to harvest a pepper is not always the easiest question to answer. It depends on the variety and ultimately what you intend to do with the fruit. For instance, it is very difficult to get jalapeños to turn red on the plant.

Almost as important as *when* to harvest is *how* to harvest. Hot peppers can burn your fingers, and wearing gloves can often damage the fruit. There are countless methods of preserving peppers, and this includes, but is not limited to, drying, smoking, pickling, roasting, freezing and making them into jellies.

For hot peppers, drying is the most popular way of preserving. Peppers can be difficult to dry in climates that are humid, since there is a problem with mold and mildew. Food dehydrators are ideal for this purpose, and it should be remembered that other fruits and vegetables can also be dehydrated. An oven on low heat also makes a good makeshift dehydrator if you do not live in a desert or dry climate. Some gardeners have luck picking the whole pepper plant and hanging it upside-down in a warm area of the house. The leaves tend to draw moisture away from the fruit, which tends to dry quickly using this method. As a general rule, the thicker the pepper

wall, such as a jalapeño, the harder it will be to dry. You can also string peppers using a needle and thread, and then hang them to dry. They make a very decorative addition to any cook's kitchen. Pickling methods and recipes abound, and most cookbooks that explain how to preserve foods will give recipes in this regard.

Freezing is another alternative, and many gardeners simply wash, dry and freeze the peppers. It is important that the peppers are in plastic bags or containers which are tightly sealed, lest the flavor invade other foods in your refrigerator. I freeze hot peppers this way, and chop them while still frozen so I can use them in cooking the same way I would use a fresh pepper.

There are other ways to preserve peppers, and if you grow them to any extent, it might be wise to invest in a book that shows the multitude of ways in which to do so. Many of the preservation methods reflect different cultures around the world. In Bermuda, for example, the standard method for preservation is to keep the chile peppers in a jar or bottle filled with sherry. Other cultures store peppers in vinegar or oil, or even vodka.

Houseplant Peppers

The criteria that make a pepper an ideal houseplant are not well defined. I was first introduced to the idea of growing peppers indoors when I visited a friend at a northern university. A classmate of his from Mexico had started growing hot pepper varieties indoors from seeds that were sent to him by his parents back home. He planted the peppers in a sunny window, hand pollinated them, and was able to produce abundant crops so that he could continue to flavor his favorite dishes and feel a little less detached from his homeland.

Many gardeners think nothing of growing some herbs indoors. Peppers are ideal, especially if you are growing a very hot variety, since it takes so little to spark up a dish. Pepper plants are also a perfect size for container plants. I have one novelty pepper plant that is nearly three years old which I move indoors in the autumn and outdoors when the warm weather returns. Indoors, I have to pollinate the flowers to get fruit, but other than that, the pepper plant does very well, especially if pruned in the autumn to compensate for lower light levels and then allowed to slowly acclimatize to outdoor life in the spring.

Medicinal and Other Uses

Peppers are rich in vitamins A, B, C and E and are also a source of potassium and niacin. Besides being classified as a vegetable (they are actually a fruit), they are also classified as an herb. They have been prescribed by herbalists for a number of ailments including asthma, colds, digestive problems, pain and toothaches.

Research has shown that many varieties of peppers have healing qualities, especially as a pain reliever and digestive aid. When taken internally, hot peppers stimulate the flow of saliva and secretions in the stomach. When rubbed on the skin, capsaicin (a red pepper derivative) preparations were thought to take the focus away from pain by being a counter-irritant. However, studies have proven that hot peppers can interfere with pain messages to the brain. There are some creams containing capsaicin that have FDA approval and can be purchased over the counter.

Hot peppers have been the topic of several on-going studies. One recent study found that candy made with hot peppers can help chemotherapy patients offset the effects of the harsh treatment they undergo. Yale University School of Medicine researchers conceived a formula for making candy from hot chili peppers in order to ease mouth pain in cancer patients. The taffy candy contains capsaicin, which is the active ingredient in hot peppers to provide control of pain after repeated applications.

Chemotherapy works by killing rapidly growing cells in the body, and unfortunately some of these include cells in the mucous membranes of the mouth and esophagus, resulting in painful sores and problems with swallowing. This usually causes nutritional problems. It is estimated that 40 to 70% of cancer therapy patients suffer from oral pain which impedes speech and eating. The new chile candy provides tactile stimulation in the mouth and the sugar inhibits the burn of capsaicin in the mouth. Traditional treatment for the pain has been local anesthetics. However, these decrease the patient's ability to eat. Researchers are now working on developing a chile-based mouthwash and ice cream for patients with difficulty in swallowing.

Studies are also ongoing concerning the probability that hot peppers may help cut cholesterol and aid in the prevention of heart disease.

Hot peppers have also been in the news lately because they are the prime ingredient in pepper sprays which police use to subdue criminals. One burst to the eyes can render a victim incapacitated for minutes, but does not inflict permanent damage. So powerful are pepper sprays that they are one of the few self-defense items that will actually protect the user from a grizzly bear attack. Because of its power to incapacitate its victim, the use and possession of pepper spray in many jurisdictions has been made illegal. One must be careful when handling hot peppers not to rub one's eyes and to wash carefully, or great pain and discomfort can result.

Potatoes

Probably the best way to grow potatoes is to choose some of the very early varieties that you can sell at a premium price while prices are still high. In addition, the earlier the potatoes, the less time you have to spend maintaining them before harvesting them. There are some truly interesting little known varieties that are blue and red. If you have the space and the time, potatoes are heavy yielding, and there is always a good market for new potatoes. If you have never tasted potatoes fresh from the soil, you don't know the treat that you are missing.

Radish

Fast to grow and healthy to eat, radishes also come in many shapes and colors. Some varieties can be ready in as little as three weeks. I use radishes to mark rows that I have planted with other seeds. Since the radishes are fast to emerge, they mark the rows. As I harvest them, the cavities they leave help aerate the soil for the remaining crop. Again, there is a large selection of radishes, including the larger winter radishes that are ideal for storage.

Squash

There are basically two types of squash: summer squash and winter squash. Probably the most common summer squash is zucchini, which can be ready in about 7 weeks. If you continually harvest the fruit, they will continue bearing throughout the season. I make a great deal of zucchini bread which I freeze and use year-round. I also find that something magical happens when you barbecue this vegetable.

Winter squashes are among some of the best storage vegetables. Some varieties of winter squash can keep almost a year if properly stored. I usually peel, seed and boil my squash and freeze the tasty flesh. I also try to have several hundred pounds stored for fresh use. I find that acorn or butternut squash are quick to prepare. I simply cut them in half, remove the seeds and add pepper and butter and maple syrup or sugar. I either microwave or bake them and they are ready in no time. They can also be stuffed with leftover hamburger meat, tuna casserole or other mixtures such as chopped apples and nuts.

Squash comes in all shapes and sizes. Some varieties can keep for almost a year when stored properly.
(Martin P. Waterman photo.)

Tomatoes

Tomatoes are one of the greatest vegetables in existence even though scientifically they are classified as a fruit. Besides being a very nutritious food, tomatoes lend themselves to various storage methods including canning, drying and freezing. The number of recipes that can be canned using tomatoes is almost limitless and includes ketchup, barbecue sauce, chili, juice and pasta sauce.

Big Beef, an award winning Tomato.
(All-America Selections photo.)

Assemble the catalogs of a few major seed companies and you will have hundreds of varieties from which to choose. The best strategy is a mix of early, mid-season and late varieties. Certain varieties keep better than others. Note that there are some newer varieties that have been bred specifically to have ultra-high levels of vitamins.

Tomatoes are one of the easiest vegetables to grow and they are highly productive. If you live in a cool climate, you can use a greenhouse or cold frame to extend your season, and, of course, tomatoes can be grown year-round indoors using hydroponic and other systems.

Other Vegetables, Specialty Crops and Exotic Vegetables

There are many other vegetables that I have not mentioned such as cucumbers, turnips, okra and leeks. The best thing is to introduce yourself to the wide selection available and continually experiment and test new varieties.

Some gardeners have even made money growing edible flowers to sell to high-class restaurants. There is also money to be made in selling fresh cut flowers, but this can be competitive and risky since similar products are often flown in from developing countries.

Mushroom growing is an area that is undergoing growth due to an expanding, robust market and the high value of this nutritious crop.

Another area worth considering both for your own use and as a potential cash crop is Chinese vegetables, and there are many of them. Ancient crops are finding their way to North American gardens from China, the former Soviet Union and South America. These will be discussed in another chapter.

Generalize vs. Specialize

The more types of vegetables you grow, the more you will be guaranteed a good crop. It is natural that you will find certain crops with which you find an affinity due to taste or ease of use and storage. There is nothing wrong with focusing on certain crops for the majority of your vegetable production. Just remember that it is a good idea to keep experimenting and not to have all your eggs in one basket. Another thing to remember is that in addition to bringing a level of security, gardening should also bring you financial and spiritual enrichment.

Recommended Reading

Vegetables: How to Select, Grow and Enjoy by Derek Fell. HP Books, Inc., 1982. ISBN 0-89586-106-2. Basic information on how to grow 80 vegetables and 28 herbs. 500 color photographs and illustrations plus much helpful information.

Grow Your Own Chinese Vegetables by Gerri Harrington. Storey Communications, Inc., 1984. ISBN 0-88266-369-0. Learn how to grow, harvest and prepare forty Chinese vegetables.

Chapter Four

Growing Fruit and Nuts

For survival gardening purposes, I like to divide fruit into two different categories, one being the berries and the second being the tree fruit. As a general rule, I look at berries as short-term investments with a quick payoff and tree fruit as longer-term investments since they can take many years to deliver their large dividends. Of course, there are some grey areas, but the idea is to think in terms of how expediently a particular plant will be able to begin the fruit production phase of its growing cycle.

In virtually all instances, fruit is a high-value crop, especially since it tends to be seasonal, tasty, nutritious, always in demand and lends itself to numerous preservation and culinary options. Many types of fresh fruit tend to be more perishable than vegetables, and this also contributes to a higher market value being placed on many varieties of fruit. For instance, one reason that raspberries are rarely seen at the supermarket is that they are extremely perishable; hence their high prices when they are available.

Fruit often suffers from the inaccurate perception that because it is a premium product, it must be difficult to grow. While it is true that some fruit crops tend to be more likely attacked by birds and other pests, they are no more difficult to grow than vegetables. If you do some homework and choose what is best for your area, as well as picking a wide selection of varieties, you will always be guaranteed an abundant crop.

Small Fruit & Berries

Strawberries, currants, gooseberries, grapes, blackberries, raspberries, huckleberries and other small fruit plants will all produce crops relatively quickly, many in their first year. You can, for instance, purchase two- and three-year-old gooseberry plants to speed up your harvest, but you will be paying a premium price for older material. This approach might be uneconomical because larger plants are not always healthy, while the shock of transplanting them may even set them back a year, since it could take a year for new roots to develop to support the vegetative growth that is above the ground.

Currants are an easy-to-grow fruit ideally suited to cooler climates.
(Martin P, Waterman photo.)

It is best to choose young, healthy material that is ideally suited to your area. It is also a wise idea to choose fruit varieties that you like.

One of the problems of the survival movement is that many believe they are destined to subsist on boring and tasteless military or dehydrated food should a natural disaster or war occur. This need not be the case, and this is an element that needs some adjustment in thinking. Unfortunately, hardship is much too often associated with the ability to survive. This is a contradiction in terms, since proper planning and preparations should eliminate hardship so that you can have continuity of your lifestyle (or even an improvement) despite factors that are outside your control.

Your hardiness zone will dictate the types of fruit that you can grow and eat. Although your local garden centers and nurseries will have many varieties that are ideal for your area, try not limit your choices. There are thousands of types of fruit, and many obscure yet high-quality and high-producing species can be purchased from some of the nurseries that specialize in searching the world for these under utilized and lesser known varieties. Although many of them are unheard of here, in their native countries they are as popular as apples, cherries and peaches are here.

Hardy Kiwi can be grown throughout North America. Many new varieties have been imported and bred.
(Martin P. Waterman photo.)

It is not difficult to grow an abundance of small fruit. Certain varieties such as raspberries and blackberries can spread so quickly that they will invade other areas of your garden.

The best way to grow small fruit is to try many of the different cultivars of the kind you choose. For instance, if you decide on raspberries, try a dozen

varieties for evaluation purposes. Then you can select the best ones to propagate based on yield, flavor, marketability, disease and pest resistance, heat and cold tolerance or whatever criteria you feel are important.

Growing many types of fruit also has its advantages. In addition to guaranteeing you a crop, you have the benefit of prolonging the time when you can enjoy fresh fruit. For instance, early in the season I enjoy currants and gooseberries. This is followed by strawberries, then raspberries and then finally blueberries, kiwi, grapes, pears and elderberries. I grow other types of small fruit as well, but the point is that if I grew only one type of fruit, it would all ripen at once. I would have to devote much time to harvesting and preserving, which would make me feel that I was supporting the garden and not the other way around. Also, some pests and diseases only occur at certain points in the growing season. By having fruit that ripens at different times, some of your harvest will not coincide with the feeding stage of a bothersome insect's life.

There have been many improvements in some small fruits such as the abilities to be everbearing and to withstand different temperature extremes. Disease and pest-resistant varieties are being released, so it is a good idea to investigate what varieties are suitable for your purposes.

This new edible fruit is a hybrid between a Mountain Ash and a Pear tree. Breeders are continually developing new and improved fruit cultivars.
(U.S.D.A. photo.)

Many fruit varieties come in early, mid-season and late varieties. This way you can plant a mixture of varieties in order to extend your season for fresh fruit. By choosing everbearing and a selection of varieties with different ripening times, you will be less prone to insect and pest attacks since your harvest will not be vulnerable to a particular insect's life cycle.

Small Fruit: Case Study — Grapes

One of the best small fruits is the grape, since it can be grown in practically all areas of North America. They are always a high-value crop and offer many alternatives for storage in the form of preserves or raisins.

In the last few decades, many fruit varieties have undergone dramatic change due to improvements. It takes an adjustment in thinking so that you can get the benefit from these positive changes. For instance, through grape breeding and better cultural practices, 40 of 50 states now boast wine industries that use domestically produced grapes. Wine and table grapes can be grown in all the states, and this includes Alaska and Hawaii.

The author's first backyard vineyard on an urban lot.
The thirty grape vines now produce about
500 pounds of grapes.
(Martin P. Waterman photo.)

As it happens, North America is blessed with many native varieties. While these native varieties provided ample food for the Native Americans and European settlers, their best use has been as an aid in breeding with high-quality grapes originating in Europe, Asia and the Middle East. In these matches between Old World and New World grapes and their

hybrids, the best of both worlds are being bred into grapes ideally suited for our North American climate.

This is often necessary, since grapes originating from outside this continent tend to be finicky and prone to diseases, pests, stress from temperature extremes and other maladies, while the North American grapes are naturally well-adapted to our climate. There is nothing wrong with cultivating wild grapes, and many people choose to do so, but there are now improved cultivars that have the hardiness and disease resistance of the wild varieties along with the benefits of a dramatic improvement in flavor.

Regardless of the variety, grapes can be used for wine, fresh eating, raisins, jellies, jams and preserves. They can also be added to many meals and desserts. Craft people have an affinity with the vine, since the canes can be used to make baskets or Christmas wreaths.

Seyval Blanc is a popular wine grape for Northern States.
It is also a great tasting dessert grape and makes
an excellent juice and jelly.
(Martin P. Waterman photo.)

There are two pieces of advice I give anyone who wants to grow grapes. First, do not pay much attention to the uses that are traditionally associated with a variety. I have grown hundreds of varieties of grapes, and one of my first mistakes was to allow other people and their perceptions to influence my grape growing. For instance, I grow many wine grapes. For the most part, many of them will never see the inside of a wine bottle because the same characteristics that make wine grapes excellent for making wine, such as high sugar and intense fruity flavors, also make them far tastier than most table grapes.

Wine grapes are rarely sold for eating because they usually have straggly clusters and small berries. For wine grapes, a higher concentration of skin to pulp is desirable since the skin contains most of the flavor and color. Another reason that you may never get to taste wine grapes is that they command a much higher price than charged for table grapes. Conversely, many dessert or eating grapes make wines that most people feel excel over the "overoaked" and much touted French and California vintages. Homemade wines are some of the best wines I have tasted, many of them coming from non-traditional grape varieties, the thought of which would make a wine connoisseur cringe. Also, wine grapes make some of the best juices available on this planet. They are also excellent when mixed with apple cider or other juices that you may be making from cull apples or other fruit. The grape juices are so intense that it does not take much to add their flavor to juice or jam mixtures.

The other piece of advice is try as many varieties as you can and then keep the ones that do best in your area. Grapes are easy to propagate from dormant cuttings, and a single mature vine can provide enough cuttings for over 100 new vines.

Try not to grow commercial varieties. In the majority of cases, they are usually only grown for characteristics that make them tough enough to endure handling and storage. They also tend to be very neutral flavored in order to please a wide group of tastes. Grapes can mimic almost any fruit flavor. Riesling has hints of apple while Cabernet Sauvignon is often compared to black currants. Each grape has its own individual flavor and personality. When I give some of my more flavorful or muscat grape varieties to people to taste, they usually say that they had no idea a grape could be so packed with flavor.

Commercial grapes also tend to have small berries. Commercial growers do not like large berries and clusters. For the home gardener, however, large clusters and berries are welcomed. Some varieties (when cluster thinned) can produce breathtaking 5-pound clusters a foot and a half in length. It pays to take some time to test a number of varieties to find the ideal grape vines that are most likely to serve your needs.

Since all grape varieties and their hybrids are descended from wild stock, their needs are not elaborate. Once you understand a few basic principles about grape growing, you can become a competent backyard viticulturist.

There are some basic rules to growing grapes that relate to planting, site selection, pruning, training and disease control. Grapes can be planted in the spring or the fall. If planted in the spring, you can use bare-rooted material as long as the vine is dormant and the roots are not allowed to dry out.

Beta grapes can take temperatures of -35F and colder and still produce a good crop.
(Martin P. Waterman photo.)

Grapes can be successfully planted in the autumn if they are potted. Vines should be planted at least 8 feet apart because a vine after the 6th or 7th year can become very large. Many of the newer vines, once established, become quite vigorous. When planting your vine, remember it has to be carefully removed from the pot and placed in a hole which has been prepared for it, using a good loose soil mix and some moisture. Unless the vine is severely root bound, care should be taken not to disturb the roots unless the vine is dormant. If the hole is dry, it will act as a wick and remove moisture from the vine, so be sure to moisten the sides and bottom of the hole. The hole should be large enough so that the new vine will have at least one and a half to two feet of loose soil in all directions in order for the roots to expand.

In the autumn, even though the vine will become dormant and shed its leaves, its roots will continue to take up nutrients until the very cold weather arrives. In the spring, the roots will become active again before the buds begin to sprout. Even though the vine may appear barren and dormant above ground, the roots will be busy growing and gathering nutrients. By spring, the vine will be on its way to becoming established. This is important because the grower has a vine that is better prepared to survive summer droughts than a vine planted in the spring. In addition, by planting a vine in the fall, fruiting can often be advanced by a full year. Furthermore, a vine that is healthier is in a better position to fight off the pressures of pests and diseases.

With site selection, there are three very important rules to follow. Choose a location to maximize the sun's light and establish good air and water drainage. Any area that will reflect heat is of extra value. Try growing a vine against a wall, a fence, or near a patio and you will be able to speed ripening and decrease the negative effects of winter.

Many new seedless grape varieties are being released such as Lakemont Seedless.
(Martin P. Waterman photo.)

Air drainage serves two purposes. The first, if you happen to live outside the southernmost parts of the United States, is that it will give a degree of frost protection. Frost flows like a river seeking lower altitudes. Therefore, do not plant grapes at the bottom of a hill or valley unless there is a large body of water

nearby capable of retaining heat. The other type of air drainage is a good steady breeze. Grapes that are grown where there is good air circulation are less likely to succumb to mildews.

Water drainage is also important. By planting your grapes on a hill for good frost drainage, you may also be able to have good water drainage. Grapes will not tolerate growing in wet, poorly drained areas.

All grapes need to be pruned. All grape varieties, including California table grapes and classic wine grapes, are descended from wild grapes. In the wild, grapes rarely fruit. Most of the vine's energy goes towards vegetative growth instead of fruit production. By pruning as much as 80% of the old growth away, you are mega-forcing nutrients and growth into fewer buds, and the results are annual fruit production. Grapes have always been known as great producers. Some varieties in California will produce over 25 tons per acre. In some markets, wine can be purchased cheaper than milk or orange juice.

Two-year-old grape vine in the author's backyard vineyard.
(Martin P. Waterman photo.)

Grapes, whether they are wild or cultivated varieties, have a natural habit of being climbers, so they will naturally climb a tree, trying to reach sunlight, and thus can easily grow over 100 feet in height. Of course, this result is not desired. When you prune a grape vine, you may have to cut off as much as two-thirds to three-quarters of the fruitful buds.

There are hundreds of pruning methods available, and you can find a good argument for the usage of almost all of them. However, there is one constant rule to follow. For most vines that are over three years old, you should prune them so that 30 buds remain, plus 10 extra buds for each additional pound of wood that you remove. The first year the vine should be pruned to form one or two trunks. Vines with two trunks or multiple trunks are becoming popular. In New York State, growers have found that a vine trained to two or more trunks will always have one trunk survive in those exceptionally cold winters that can happen every few decades or so.

The shaping that you use will depend on the purpose you have in mind for your vines. All vines need some type of support. Increasingly, this support comes in the form of some type of training. Grapes can be trained to cover arbors, walls, chain link fences, archways and, of course, trellises. A short trellis in the backyard makes a useful backyard divider, and in the summer when it is covered with foliage and fruit, also acts as a convenient privacy hedge. If you plan to grow several grapes on a trellis, most books on pruning will provide a number of different methods for training grapes in a vineyard.

The basic way to grow grapes organically is to choose a good site, select several varieties of disease-resistant vines and hope for the best. Fortunately, many of the new grapes have a great deal of disease resistance.

The major problems with grapes come from mildews, but these can be controlled with sulfur sprays. Many of the newer varieties are superior at resisting mildews. Some kinds of grapes at the supermarket seem to have so much sulfur spray residue left on them that I suppose that you could use them to make gunpowder.

In the autumn, when most of the rains come, a favorable environment is created for the development of mildews. If you choose early ripening grapes such as the ones recommended in this chapter, you may be able to grow no-spray grapes unless you are in a very humid area. However, mildews late in the season seem to benefit a vine. I have talked to several grape growers and breeders who have told me that when you spray a vine late in the season, the vine has a tendency to put out new succulent growth. This depletes the vine of nutrients and this new growth is killed during the winter. By not spraying the mildews, you help to defoliate the vines, which will slow down their growth and help mature good dark wood, thus helping them to survive the winter.

A good strategy is to grow a variety of different grapes. This way, statistically, most will not be affected by weather, insects or diseases in the same season.

Tree Fruit

There are some ways to get around the problem of tree fruit taking a long time to begin production. For instance, most fruit trees when planted on a dwarfing rootstock will fruit many years earlier than if grown on their roots; some during their very first year.

Freshly harvested peaches.
(U.S.D.A. photo.)

Just because you are growing tree fruit does not mean you will have to go without fruit harvests. Many commercial and small growers use some of these quicker growing fruit bearing plants to intercrop when they are planting tree crops. For instance, if you are installing an apple or peach orchard, it will not produce for several years. However, if you plant strawberries between the rows, you can be harvesting crops while you wait for the trees to begin their full production.

Tree Fruit Case Study — The Apple

The most popular tree fruit in North America is the apple. However, the apple tree that most people envision has undergone dramatic change. We tend to picture the apple tree as being large, spreading and stately. Most people familiar with apple trees will also agree that they are a welcome addition to the garden if you have the space and the time to spray them. This is certainly true, if one is speaking of the traditional varieties that have always been grown in the past. But, if one considers the new apple trees that are now available, some dramatic rethinking is required.

You will never find these varieties or this type of selection of apples at your local supermarket.
(U.S.D.A. photo.)

In a world where everything is going high-tech and new and improved, it was probably inevitable that this sort of thinking would spill over into horticulture and bring about the development of superior fruit trees.

There have been two major improvements that make the apple tree ideal for the garden and smaller spaces. The first is the additional progress that has been made in improving the selection and performance of dwarfing rootstocks. Since it was discovered that almost any variety of apple could be grafted onto a crab apple rootstock to produce a dwarfing tree, many improvements have followed. One of these improvements is that many dwarf rootstocks are able to withstand very cold temperatures. Because many of our favorite apple trees have roots that are too tender for some areas of the North, these dwarf rootstocks have been instrumental in producing trees that are hardy and an ideal size for smaller spaces. The dwarfing rootstocks have been further improved in breeding programs, and we now have rootstocks that will produce a tree of various low heights.

This dwarf apple tree is loaded with fruit. The fruit is easily harvested and the tree is easily pruned and maintained. Best of all, no long wait for the tree to begin fruiting.
(Martin P. Waterman photo.)

Most varieties of apple trees grown on their own roots can reach very large proportions. Many remember the giant old trees on the old farm that as a youngster you had to learn to climb in order to get an apple. With a dwarf tree, you can often fit a dozen or more of them in the space that a standard size apple tree would occupy. Another advantage of the dwarf tree is that almost all the fruit is within easy reach for picking without the use of a ladder. The shorter height makes pruning, grafting, spraying and other duties very easy to perform.

A most delightful feature in using a dwarf rootstock is that the tree will bear fruit earlier. It is not unusual for apple trees grafted on to dwarf rootstocks to bear apples as early as the first or second year after receiving the tree from the nursery. If it does bear in the first year, it may be better to remove most of the young fruit from these trees because at this tender age fruiting will come at the expense of growth. A standard tree can often take as long as eight years to begin to produce fruit.

The second improvement, and probably the most exciting, concerns spraying apple trees. Spraying is an inconvenience because of the time involved and the necessity of repeat applications, particularly after wet weather. In addition, in these times of environmental and health concerns, most people do not like the idea of spraying chemicals on apples to control diseases such as mildew, rust and scab.

The improvement which has many excited is the development of scab-free apples. Scab in not only damaging to the fruit, it can also reduce vigor in the tree. For almost five decades, universities and research stations have been working on scab-free apples, and the first crop of releases has proven itself to be worthy of all the early hype and excitement.

Breeding a scab-free apple was easy; it was just a matter of exposing all the different varieties to the disease and then working with the ones that survived. Unfortunately, the survivors were not of commercial quality. The big challenge in breeding became improved quality, which now has been attained. Varieties are continually being tested for improved quality to see if they merit future release.

There are, of course, other benefits in growing scab-free dwarf apple trees in the garden. A dwarf tree will produce 20-40 pounds of apples. You can grow a selection of different flavors and types in a fraction of the space that a standard tree would occupy. Apples that are allowed to ripen on the tree are tastier than those in the store because the tree ripened apples have a higher sugar content and a more developed flavor. So, by combining these two innovations, you can select your own designer trees by choosing the quality of apple you want and the size of the tree that you require.

Subtropical Berries and Tree Fruit

Many varieties of fruit that have often been associated with subtropical or tropical climates are becoming available in hardier forms. For instance, citrus has undergone a dramatic change owing to new cultivars that can take colder temperatures and are ever-expanding the range northward. While some of the newer banana cultivars could not compete with fruit from banana producing countries, some exotic varieties that are unavailable in supermarkets could command a premium price. Don't limit your options

to fruit plants that are standards. Experiment and have fun trying different varieties from outside your area and around the world. It could be the start of something really exciting. There is still much pioneering work to be done in the area of growing new varieties of fruit.

Nut Trees

One of the great things about nut trees is that when they decide to fruit, they can fruit in abundance. However, many will not be annual producers, and the wait for some of the larger species can be over a decade. On the other side of the coin, nuts have a very long storage life and are packed with nutrition.

Many of the nut trees are native to North America and grow over a wide range. Some nuts that you may wish to consider growing are butternuts, black walnuts, chestnuts, pecans, hazelnuts and filberts.

Recommended Reading

Tree Fruit Production by Benjamin J.E. Teskey. AVI Publishing Company, Inc., 1982. ISBN 0-87055-265-1. If you want to grow apples, pears, peaches, cherries, plums, apricots or nectarines, this book is a very thorough text on the subject.

Tropical Fruits by J.A. Samson. Longman Scientific & Technical, 1986. ISBN 0-470-20679. If you are blessed with a warm climate, this book will show you how to grow the popular varieties (bananas, citrus, etc.) as well as new and minor crops such as kiwi, litchi, passion fruit and feijoa.

Temperate-Zone Pomology: Physiology and Culture by Melvin Neil Westwood. Timber Press, Inc., 1993. ISBN 0-88192-253-6. An excellent text for anyone who is involved in fruit growing.

Chapter Five

Growing Herbs and Medicinal Plants

Before we discuss herbs and medicinal plants, you should consider the fact that while foods are not technically drugs, they can serve most of the same purposes. For example, protein from food such as beans can give you bursts of energy, while carbohydrates such as those contained in fresh vegetables or pastas can often make you feel tired or sluggish. Sugars can have a dramatic effect on your body, as can many other components that are found in everyday foods. This is something you should be aware of when you contemplate the health benefits of fresh fruits and vegetables as well as herbs and medicinal plants. Athletes and sports medicine doctors are conscious of the healing and energy power of certain foods, and many who take note of the curative and restorative properties of certain foods structure their diets to include these natural sources of nutrition and medication.

Unfortunately, the common perception is one which stereotypes medicinal plants and herbs as being New Age medicines, and some sort of recent creation. They do not realize that Chinese medicine as well as the medical practices of the native people of North America, predates European medicine by centuries. There are many people who argue that this older style of medicine is, in many respects, still far in advance of the type of Western medicine that is practiced today. Of course, modern day medicine has come under much scrutiny since it tends to treat the effects of an illness and not the cause. Therefore, people often become dependent on medication and use this as an unnatural substitute for good nutrition, exercise and other preventative measures. There is also much concern that a large percentage of

prescription drugs as well as non-prescription drugs can do more harm than good.

In the United States, it is estimated that as much as 75% of all diseases are diet-related. In addition, it is also estimated that 35% of all cancer cases could be prevented if a more healthy diet was commonplace. It seems that every week there is a new study released extolling the health virtues of a balanced diet consisting of fresh fruit and vegetables.

Our society is one that feasts on foods which are nutritionally deficient. Our typical diets are high in saturated fats, refined sugars and cereals, meats and other animal products. Most of the processed foods that many of us eat lack fiber and nutrients and, in many cases, are very detrimental to our physical (and thus mental) health.

For instance, one recent study conducted in Boston has shown that a diet low in fruits can be very damaging to your health. In the study, two groups of healthy people, aged 60 to 100, were fed various amounts of food rich in vitamin C. The study found that there exists a strong relationship between elevated blood pressure and either low intakes or low blood levels of this vitamin that is found in many fresh fruits and vegetables. Scientists are still analyzing this discovery, and are not sure if other vitamins and minerals are also responsible for the reduction of blood pressure.

The vegetables and fruits with the highest vitamin C content are tomatoes, peppers, strawberries and leafy green vegetables. As you plan your garden, you may want to take the health benefits of these foods into consideration.

You may also want to pick up a book on nutrition so that you can gain a better understanding of the various types of fruits and vegetables that can help you to improve and maintain good health.

With fears over cuts in health care growing, people are beginning to focus on preventative health care methods. If you truly want to be self-sufficient, you should consider how dependent you are on your doctor, medicine chest and pharmacy, and how you can change this dependency. It is a well-proven fact that a more natural lifestyle can help free you from dependencies on drugs and medical care. At the very least, your dependencies will be lessened and your garden will provide a natural source of vitamins, medications and healing foods.

Gardening and growing healthy foods that can be preserved and eaten year-round is a strong step in the right direction. Many books on preserving victuals will inform you about which methods are best in maintaining a high vitamin content when you store foods for long periods of time.

When you study seed catalogs, you may notice that many varieties have been specifically bred to offer higher levels of vitamins such as A and C.

I know many gardeners in their eighties or nineties and I have always wondered what the secret was to their longevity. I used to think it was the exercise that gardening provided, but now I am sure that their healthy diets also have a bearing on their long lives.

Growing a plant that provides both food and medicine can be a rewarding endeavor. It also has the benefit of being a food that you grow and prepare which needs not be treated with pesticides, which can damage your immune system.

Herbs

There are so many types of herbs which you can grow that you are best advised to do some homework in this regard. The best way to get started is to test a number of the most popular herbs. These are widely available and there are many specialty companies that sell nothing but herbs.

There has been an explosion of books on herbal remedies and cures, and many of these can be ordered from the sources in the appendix.

To help you decide which herbs to grow, you should become familiar with their uses. Some herbs make excellent teas. Other herbs are ideal for seasoning food. Many herbs can be used to make natural cosmetics, and still other herbs are in demand

to treat practically any ailment from insomnia to impotence.

You should also investigate those herbs which can be dried or preserved in different ways so that they can be stored for long periods of time.

Every garden should contain an herbal section. Besides the fact that herbs can help turn your survival rations into gourmet food, they also offer a degree of nutrition.

While many herbs do not really offer much in the way of substance as far as putting bulk foods away, they can be a good revenue producer. Fresh basil, parsley and rosemary are always in demand. Many small growers do well selling fresh herbs to restaurants and grocery stores, as well as selling bedding plants to gardeners and other growers. Fresh herbs can also be sold as value-added products because many lend themselves to container gardening, window boxes and hanging baskets. This allows gardeners in apartments or on small lots an opportunity to have a supply of fresh herbs for cooking. Dried herbs can also command high prices if you package and market them yourself.

Herb Case Study
— The Mints

Everyone can recognize the distinct taste of mint. It is in our toothpaste, mouthwash, meals, candy and even medicine. Yet for all its fame, mint remains mysterious and misunderstood.

Several reasons account for our unfamiliarity with respect to this popular herb. Mint is very easy to grow; so much so, that it often grows on its own to the point where many gardeners have trouble containing the invasive plants. Obviously, if this herb were more difficult to grow, like finicky ginseng, it would probably be extolled as being far more precious and thus worthy of greater study and appreciation.

Understanding mints can often be confusing. We can deduce that apple mint, orange mint, peppermint and spearmint are mints, but few realize that rosemary, lavender, sage, thyme, salvia and lemon balm are also considered mints and they all belong to the same family, *Labiate*.

Another reason for misunderstanding mint is the sheer number of varieties that exist. In fact, there are more than six hundred varieties of mint. With such a selection and so many variations, there comes a wider spectrum of applications and uses for herbal mints that few gardeners may have contemplated.

Gaining an in-depth knowledge of all the varieties and their idiosyncratic personalities can be a daunting task, to say the least. However, once you understand some of the uses of mint, you will be in a better position to see how this herb can fit into your growing plans. It is surprising just how many uses there are for mint. For instance, mint has been the topic of numerous news stories recently because of its proven track record of being a viable and safe insect repellent.

When most people talk about mints, they are referring to the genus *Mentha*. For those who may be lured into exploring mints for pleasure or profit, it is important to note that mint classification can be confusing, to say the least. When I refer to mints I will be referring to the most popular members of the genus *Mentha* and those varieties that are most often considered as true mints.

Mint History

With so many uses and so many species, it is not surprising that mint has a long and fascinating history.

It is accepted that mint was widely used and distributed in the Middle East. So valued was mint that it could be used for the payment of taxes. Mint is referred to several times in the Bible and it is suspected that the mint mentioned in the Bible is *Mentha longifolia,* or horse mint, which is still widely distributed throughout the region.

Mint spread to Greece and became established in Greek mythology. The god Pluto fell in love with Minthe, a beautiful nymph. Pluto's wife, Persephone, became jealous and turned Minthe into mint. Pluto could not turn Minthe back into a living form, so he gave her a fragrant aroma.

Both the Greeks and Romans added mint to milk in an effort to prevent spoilage. It is interesting to note that mint was far more popular in Roman times than it is today. Marcus Gabius Apicius, a famous chef in his day (14-37 AD), mentions dried or fresh mint on practically every page of his book on cookery.

Herbalists from China to Germany to England have extolled the virtues of mint as a medicinal herb throughout the centuries.

Until 1696, all mints were regarded as one plant. This was changed when British botanist John Ray began to divide them into separate species.

In the early 1880s, peppermint oil was first distilled to produce menthol. This menthol found applications as treatments for burns, scalds and insect bites, and in chest rubs that were used to relieve asthma, hay fever and morning sickness.

The two most important mints are peppermint and spearmint. Peppermint is a relatively recent introduction which is suspected as being a hybrid of spearmint and water mint, resulting in a natural hybrid of spearmint species.

Modern and Commercial Uses

Several countries have substantial acreage devoted to the growing of mint. These countries include the United States, Australia, Brazil, India and Japan. Spearmint and peppermint are the two most popular mints that are grown in the United States. Much of the mint is grown in the Pacific Northwest.

Oregon is the leading producer of mint in the United States, with over 45,000 acres in production. The Oregon climate is particularly favorable, with a long growing season, moist cool winters and good soils which produce some of the highest-quality mint oil in the world. This allows Oregon to provide over 40 percent of the U.S. market.

Once planted, mint remains in production from 3-15 years, although the average is about 6-7 years before replanting is required.

With commercial plantings, the mint are windrowed and allowed to dry for three to five days in the field. This curing process allows much of the moisture to escape from the plants. The harvest is conducted in late July or August. After this period of natural curing, the mint is picked up by a chopper and chopped and blown into tubs which are then taken to a distillery. The mint is steamed and the oils evaporate with the water and then condense into a mixture of water and mint oil. This mixture then passes through a separator to remove the water. Mint oil is traditionally stored in 55-gallon drums which hold about 400 pounds. (Mint oil is measured in pounds and not in gallons.) It takes approximately five and a half acres of mint to fill one 55-gallon drum. On the surface, this would appear to be a lot of labor to produce just one barrel of mint oil. But mint oil is potent, so much so that a mere pound will flavor

45,000 sticks of chewing gum. Mint oil sells for between $15 and $25 a pound, and is a valuable crop. Scientists at the U.S.D.A consider mint a possible alternative crop for Bolivian peasants who farm coca in the Andean foothills.

Culinary Uses

Mint is very versatile in the kitchen. Since the difference between the flavors of certain varieties of mint are subtle, substitutions can often be made. Spearmint is the mint of choice for traditional mint sauce or mint jelly to accompany lamb. Spearmint is also good with fresh vegetables such as peas, carrots and new potatoes. Peppermint in the West is most often used as a flavoring in such products as candy and desserts.

If you want a flavor that is not as pronounced as spearmint, you may want to substitute apple or pineapple mint.

Basil mint, which is so named because it is often mistaken for basil, has a pleasing lemon scent and can do wonders when added to cake or cookie dough.

Mint is one of the most attractive of the edible garnishes. It can be used in a number of ways that are only limited by the imagination of the food preparer.

Mint is at its very best when fresh. It will keep in the refrigerator briefly if stored in plastic bags. It can also be stored upright in a jar with a little water to slow it from losing quality.

If you must store fresh leaves for an extended amount of time, the best method is to put them in ice cube trays and add water. As you require the fresh leaves, you can thaw the mint cubes as needed. Mint leaves can also be dried but they must be kept in an airtight container in a cool and dark place. Mint plants are harvested and hung upside down. It usually takes a few weeks for them to dry. When drying mint, remember to do so in a dark place so that they can retain as much of their flavoring as possible. Dried mint is often called for with recipes that have a Middle Eastern origin.

Mint has earned the esteem of pastry chefs. The mint leaves can be crystallized and used as attractive decorations on pastries and cakes. The crystallized leaves can be served as an alternative to mints after a meal. Although time-consuming, crystallizing mint leaves is not difficult to do.

Start with one and a quarter cups of water, dissolve two ounces of gum arabic. Choose the largest and freshest mint leaves and brush the mixture on both sides of the leaves. Dip the leaves into very fine or icing sugar and make sure the complete leaf is coated. Gently shake off the excess sugar and spread out the leaves to dry on a wire rack. Allow them to dry for 24 hours and then turn them over for an additional 24 hours. When the leaves are sufficiently dry, place in an airtight container and store in a dark place.

Mints can be added to numerous dips and sauces. One of my favorite dips is made from finely chopped or puréed cucumbers, a couple of cups of unflavored yogurt and about a dozen finely chopped mint leaves. When chilled, it is an excellent appetizer or snack when served with fresh broccoli, cauliflower, celery and zucchini slices. It is also very healthy, low in calories and surprisingly filling. Mint seems to go particularly well with frozen desserts or fruit. Finely-chopped mints can also be added to ice cream.

Teas and Beverages

Mint has always been popular as a tea, but there are several variations. Iced mint tea can be very refreshing and you can spark up your hot chocolate or other chocolate drinks with the addition of mint.

Spearmint is a favorite for teas around the world, and in particular North Africa and the Middle East. Spearmint is also traditional for use with mint juleps. Mint juleps are traditionally made with bourbon.

Mint as a Pesticide

Before we talk about pesticidal uses, it is important to realize that there are some unsavory characteristics that have been attributed to mint. Fortunately, mint is mostly distasteful to certain species of insects, since it does contain ample amounts of natural pesticides.

One of the most reported methods to protect certain crops is to plant mint near broccoli, cabbage, brussels sprouts, lettuce, tomatoes and beans to discourage feeding by the cabbage loopers and cabbage worms.

Mint has a dual personality since it also has a reputation for attracting beneficial insects to the garden. Several texts recommend the planting of mint to attract these good insects and to help them become established in your garden. However, be aware that interplanting mint in your garden comes with some risks, since mint is a fast-growing plant and can quickly smother its neighbors. In other words, unless you are able to contain the mint, the solution may be worse than your original problem.

Mint will also deter insect pests from humans and their pets. Mint that has been dried and ground into a powder has been used in many herbal remedies to treat pets for fleas. Pennyroyal has a long history in folklore as an insect repellent, and another name for pennyroyal is fleabane. The Roman naturalist, Pliny, observed as early as the first century A.D. that pennyroyal would repel fleas. It will also repel mosquitoes and ticks. Many gardeners will rub pennyroyal on their skin before working outdoors. Others will hang a small satchel of the herb on their pet's collar to help discourage fleas and ticks.

Medicinal Uses

Mint has been long used for its medicinal properties. Many of the herbal applications of mint have a long history of usage, and are well established among herbalists. Many of mint's healing properties have been documented.

The oldest surviving medical text, the Egyptian *Ebers Papyrus*, lists mint as being able to soothe the stomach. The ancient Egyptians were not the only people to know the value of mint. When Europeans came to the Americas, they found that the Indians used the native mints to treat coughs and chest congestion.

Despite its positive medicinal attributes, mint has come under increased scrutiny since it can be toxic in large doses. This is particularly true with pennyroyal. Whenever we consume certain mints, we are, in fact, consuming pesticides. Therefore, some people are reluctant to grow or consume mint because they believe that it may be harmful in one manner or another. Their fears may be supported by the fact that there have been documented cases where death has occurred when massive, not just large, but *massive* amounts of mint were consumed.

Mint oil in high dosage can kill a person. However, so will coffee and other common foods. Therefore, it is important to put the toxicity issue into perspective.

It has been calculated that it would take 4,441 mg. per kg. of weight to kill a person. This means that if peppermint tea was made using ten grams of the herb, and assuming that there was complete extraction of all the oils, it would then take 444,441 grams to kill a man that weighs 100 kg or about 220 pounds. In other words, to do himself in, the man would have to consume 4,441 cups of peppermint tea. In comparison, the same male would only have to drink 192 cups of coffee in order to receive a lethal dose of caffeine.

Just how safe is mint? Several texts claim it is safe, except they caution that it is wise to stay clear of large doses for children and pregnant women. James A. Duke, an economic botanist with the National Germplasm Resources Laboratory of the U.S.D.A., has studied the pesticidal qualities of the mints. He has found that some members of the mint family, such as oregano, can contain as much as 100,000 times more natural pesticides (on a ppm basis) than synthetic pesticide residues. He learned this as he was trying to prove incorrect a theory that we consume 10,000 times more natural pesticides than synthetic residues.

Duke is studying mints that contain high levels of pulegone, a compound that is proven to repel fleas, ticks and mosquitoes. This is important since certain ticks carry the organisms responsible for Lyme disease and Rocky Mountain spotted fever.

There is no disagreement that mint has many properties that warrant additional study. Mints are generally regarded as safe by the Food and Drug Administration. The exception is for women who are pregnant or nursing. They should limit the amount of mint that they consume.

Mints are a popular ingredient in herbal home remedies and have been used for a wide spectrum of ailments. Mint is usually present in mixtures used to treat colds, fevers and chest complaints, to cure headaches and act as a sedative. It is also considered to be antiseptic and to have antibiotic properties.

The leaves and flowers of peppermint can be eaten to remove hardened mucus from the alimentary and bronchial system. Peppermint tea is good for your digestive system and will help control flatulence.

Spearmint has been long used as a diuretic and a treatment for high blood pressure. It is also considered a stimulant.

Mint has been used to prevent infection, and peppermint oil has been proven effective in killing certain types of bacteria. Mint has been applied to wounds by different societies and cultures throughout the world.

Of course, it is well known that mint will aid digestion and calm stomach unrest. This is the reason so many restaurants distribute them after a meal. This is not a recent practice. It was an ancient custom to top off a feast with a sprig of mint.

Miscellaneous Uses

Mint has been used as a beauty aid in a number of different procedures. Women have steamed their faces with peppermint by boiling leaves and putting a towel over their head to catch the steam. Peppermint tea can also be applied directly to the face by soaking a clean cloth in the tea and then applying it as a compress. Mint is suspected of having astringent qualities, which means that it acts to contract bodily tissues and thereby diminish discharges.

You can make your own mouthwash by boiling 1 teaspoon each of peppermint, rosemary and lavender to 3 cups of boiling water. After the mixture has been steeped for three minutes, it can be strained and used as a mouthwash.

If you make your own soap, peppermint oil can be added just before the mixture is poured into the molds.

It should surprise no one that a plant as widely distributed and as useful as ancient mint would become a prominent herb in magical potions. Three of its touted powers are in assisting in prosperity, protection and health. Keeping a mint leaf in your wallet or rubbing your money with mint is supposed to bring prosperity. Mint is also used in lust potions, so it's easy to see why a herb that can be used in spells to bring about love and money may be considered important in the magical trade.

Finally, many people like the smell of mint as an air freshener, particularly around Christmas. Peppermint oil can be added to your mop water to spread this fragrance throughout your kitchen.

Culture

Because mint has a tendency to grow well, you should consider carefully where you want to grow it. One consideration about mint should be whether you want it as part of the landscape or as part of the herb garden.

Mint plants are attractive and can provide ample amounts of green area quickly. Mint has square stems, opposite aromatic leaves, and small flowers, usually of a pale purple, pink or white. Because of the wide selection, they can be used for many design purposes and not just as a food plant.

Mint is a perennial herb and will tolerate partial shade. In most cases, it is a moisture-loving plant, which may explain why it grows particularly well in climates such as the Pacific Northwest. There are mint varieties that are adaptable to warm or cold climate gardening, so no gardener should have to go without mint. Mint is also very tolerant of most soils, and prefers a soil pH of between 6.0 and 8.

Propagation can be done by using runners or roots and simply planting them in pots. Mint can also be planted by using seeds, but it is important to realize that most mint will not grow true from seeds. Clumps can be divided in the spring, preferably before growth starts. Mint can also be divided and replanted in the fall. If you do not care what variety of mint you grow, you can also plant the seeds. If you intend to plant enough for regular harvests, mint should be spaced one to two feet apart.

As desirable as mint can be, there is a problem. Mint can be a very invasive plant. There are many ways to solve this problem. I prefer to use a five-gallon food service pail with the bottom removed. The pail is buried so that the rim is just slightly above ground level. How high the rim should be will depends on whether your variety spreads by underground root stolons or by the above-ground runners. If it spreads by runners, you should have the containment ring a little bit higher. Your containment system can be aesthetic, and the possibilities are endless. You can contain mint by burying bricks, placing large flag stones or even constructing a large underground container from discarded lumber, although the latter would have a limited service life.

The fast-growing fibrous root that mint exhibits has some beneficial qualities, inasmuch as it is one of those plants that has been recommended to prevent soil erosion. Mint can be used to quickly naturalize an area that may have been made barren due to construction or erosion. Mint is also one of the select group of plants that will grow well along the edge of a lawn.

For those with cramped spaces or who are apartment dwellers, mint makes an ideal container plant. It is an attractive container plant particularly if you continually harvest the leaves, since this will produce a very bushy plant. Mint should be grown in a container that allows the roots to spread about a foot in each direction. Container plants should be divided each year.

Mint does best if it gets at least an inch of water per week. If you grow mint in containers or baskets which tend to dry out quickly, you should have a vigilant watering schedule.

While many curse the invasive properties of mint, other gardeners actually welcome it. For instance, water mint is an ideal plant to naturalize a wet or boggy area of the garden. It is hardy to U.S.D.A. Zone 5, grows to two feet in height, and will produce lavender blooms in June-July. Many people like to plant water mint near a pond, since they desire a plant that will provide partial shade to help curb the growth of algae and keep the water cooler. Mint can be an important element for those who like to practice edible landscaping. Mint is an ideal edible substitute for many perennials, especially where a dark green foliage color is desired.

One of the most popular mints for the landscape is variegated apple mint. It is traditionally used along paths and for border areas. It does particularly well in soggy areas and its green and white colors add a cool look during hot summer days.

Corsican mint is an ideal plant to use between patio stones and rocks in the garden. When you step on it, it will release the familiar mint aroma. Corsican mint is one of the mints which is the least prone to spreading.

Of course, an easy way to cure yourself of the problem of mint invasion is to find enough uses for it that it is being harvested about as fast as it is spreading.

Mint can also be used in many of the classic or newer designs for a herb garden. Planting all your herbs in one area with a specific design has many practical purposes. Firstly, you can draw a map of your herb garden so that it is easy to distinguish between the various herbs that often look similar, and secondly, it can be convenient when one needs a particular mint.

After a few years of growth, most mint species will become woody. They can be dug up and new plants started from root cuttings. If a piece of root has at least one joint node, it should produce a plant.

It is best to harvest your mint before the flowers bloom, since blooming reduces the oil content of the leaves. At the end of the season, some gardeners cut their plants back to the ground to eliminate over-wintering sites for insect pests.

Several maladies are the result of mint receiving too much moisture. If this is the case, avoid over-watering the mint, or, if you water the plants, avoid splashing the leaves and water at root level. Mints are usually about as trouble-free as any plant can get. If your particular mint is giving you problems, try growing some of the other numerous varieties.

Indoor Culture

Mint is also ideally suited for indoor culture. In the home, mint should be put in an area where it will receive an adequate amount of sun. Mint will thrive in a greenhouse, but needs to be partially shaded or the heat will have a detrimental effect on the plants.

Indoor mint growing is usually practiced by those who are in U.S.D.A. Zone 4 and colder, and experience a short growing season. Container plants can be brought indoors, but will usually drop leaves and look a little sickly for a while. Mint, like all plants, receives much of its nourishment from the sun, and adjusting to an indoor environment is tantamount to putting it on a strict diet; in other words, it is going to lose some weight. You can help the adjustment by harvesting heavily from the plant before you bring it indoors.

Mint may never be as popular as it was in Roman and earlier times. Still, there is a growing interest in this herb, and that is justified by the versatility of this ancient plant.

If you have never grown mint, peppermint and spearmint are obvious choices for starters. As for uses, mint can keep you busy as you try new taste sensations. However, don't limit yourself to just a few varieties. You may want to try orange mint, which has the smell and slight taste of citrus. Chocolate mint is another mint that is quickly gaining in popularity. The stems of chocolate mint are chocolate colored and most people think the plant smells like chocolate dinner mints.

Mint is widely available as seeds and plants. Seeds are fine if you don't mind variations. Who knows, maybe you'll discover a new variety worth propagating.

Medicinal Plants

Many medicines such as antibiotics are unavailable unless you have a prescription from your doctor. However, since most pharmaceuticals are derived from plants, with a little research and understanding you can grow your own medicines and stock your medicine cabinet.

Making your own medicine is not a new fad. Many cultures have been practicing these methods since the beginning of recorded history and probably long before that.

Unfortunately, many medicines are illegal to grow. This is unlikely to change, since the medical and insurance lobbies are so powerful, and for the simple reason that there exists too large a population of bureaucrats and thinkers who believe that society should depend on government or government licensed businesses and institutions for their every need.

While probably no one will question you for making raspberry tea to aid in childbirth, you would probably face a different situation if you decided to grow effective pain killers by cultivating poppies so that you could make opium tea. Obviously, you could be breaking major laws.

Another consideration is the dosage. Many plants used in medicine can be poisonous or toxic in large amounts, and this could even lead to death. Nevertheless, there is a large population of gardeners and herbalists from all walks of life who prefer to grow their own natural healing plants.

Medicinal Plant Case Study — Aloe Vera

One prime example of a widely used medicinal plant is aloe vera. There are many people who know about the aloe vera plant and its wonderful uses. However, there are still many people who are unfamiliar with this medicinal plant and its miraculous healing qualities. This is unfortunate, because this plant can be grown indoors anywhere in North America and outdoors in many areas in the South.

Dioscorides, a Greek physician, wrote before the time of Christ of aloe vera's healing properties. Word of this plant with magical properties spread wherever men traveled. It was thought that Alexander the Great conquered Madagascar so that there would be an uninterrupted supply of aloe vera for his army to use in healing their wounds sustained in battle.

Aloe vera is native to Africa and the Mediterranean areas. It is now widely grown around the world in areas such as South America, the Bahamas, the West Indies and Egypt. In the United States it is grown in southern Florida, Arizona and Texas. Aloe vera is still used today in a wide variety of applications. The Slukari tribesmen in the African Congo still rub aloe gel all over their bodies. This is done to mask the human scent before they hunt. All over the world women apply the gel to their face to make their skin look younger and healthier, and, of course, it is probably the most effective burn cream available.

The healing properties of aloe vera have been studied in scientific laboratories, and this continues to be done both by the academic and industrial communities. Research chemists are working to develop applications for commercial products such as shampoos, creams, lotions and even foods.

Aloe vera has demonstrated that it has three strong properties. It is anesthetic (causes loss of feeling), antibacterial (prevents growth and infection from bacteria) and has the ability to aid tissues in restoring themselves to normal health. It is this restorative ability that has so many excited about aloe. If a cut or burn is not severe, aloe will help it heal quickly and leave no scar or evidence of injury. When aloe vera is applied to poison ivy rash, sun burns, blisters, insect stings and bites, it soothes the discomfort and heals the affected areas.

Some other ailments that aloe vera is reported to cure are athlete's foot, psoriasis, eczema and yeast infections.

Aloe vera has also been widely used in folk medicine cures for skin cancer and other cancers, a use that is currently under investigation by the medical community.

It has been reported that aloe vera has also been successful at clearing and controlling acne and is effective at eliminating dandruff.

The way that aloe vera is traditionally used is to cut or break off a section of one of the lower leaves. The lowest leaves are the oldest. The new leaves are always produced from the center. After you remove a section or whole leaf, slice it open and apply the gel to the intended area on your skin. If the area is large or is a major burn, you can apply the opened leaf and wrap gauze around it to make a poultice. Sometimes an area where the aloe vera has been applied will become dry. Some people mix the gel with some vitamin E or a moisturizer to avoid this effect.

Although aloe vera can be taken internally, it is not recommended. It can cause intestinal pain and has a laxative effect. It can be stabilized and taken internally, but the process of stabilization can diminish its healing abilities. Aloe vera powder (a brown powder made from the dried gel) is still mentioned in many medical texts. In addition to listing its uses, these texts warn of irritation of the kidneys. Aloe vera powder is still widely used by veterinarians.

Aloe vera will grow year-round outdoors in U.S.D.A. hardiness Zone 10. It is a popular container plant in cooler regions where it can be moved outdoors when minimum temperatures do not go below 41°F.

Aloe vera plants like a neutral soil and will tolerate a soil that is low in nutrients. Drainage is important, as they do not like a soil that is too damp. Although they do well in ordinary potting soil, they will do better if some sand is added or if you purchase a cactus type of soil. They do not require much water, but do prefer full sun. People have had success in growing them in partial sun or shade. If you grow them in a pot, they perform best when the roots are a little crowded. When you must repot, do this in the late winter or spring.

Aloe vera make ideal indoor house plants
or ideal outdoor container plants.
(Martin P. Waterman photo.)

Aloe has an aesthetic advantage; it makes an attractive ornamental plant. When the plant flowers, it sends an exotic spike-shaped flower about three feet above the plant.

Aloe vera plants show up regularly at garden centers and nurseries and have been a popular offering in the trade. It is unfortunate that so many people buy the plant without any knowledge of its healing abilities.

Aloe vera plants continually send up suckers from their roots. These should be removed when they grow over six inches in height. This can be done at repotting time. The suckers can be planted in separate pots where they will grow into new healthy plants. At any one time, I seem to have at least a dozen plants, and find I am continually giving them away as gifts.

Aloe vera plants can also be started from seeds. The seeds are formed when the plant flowers. However, it is much easier and faster to grow the plants from suckers unless you have a need for a large number of plants in a relatively short amount of time.

If you know no one who has a plant, you can order them directly from Abbey Gardens. Their address is 4620 Carpinteria Avenue, Carpinteria, California, 93013. They specialize in cactus and succulents and their catalog is only two dollars. Most plants are under $5 and they have 80 varieties of aloe, including aloe vera. Aloe vera is also becoming more and more available due to its increasing reputation for healing. Be sure to check your local greenhouses and garden centers.

Once you begin to use and depend on aloe vera, you will wonder how you ever lived without it. When I am away from my plants and find myself with a cut, burn or bad insect sting or bite, it always underscores for me how much the plants have become a medicine cabinet unto themselves.

In the future, scientists may unlock the mystery of the medicinal aloe vera and find new applications for this healing plant. In the meantime, because of its proven healing properties, no home should be without at least one plant.

Other Herb Uses

Herb vinegars are a very popular value-added product that is both healthy and nutritious. Also, many types of herbs can deter insects and pests from moving into your garden. There are hundreds of herbs that you can try, and, many rare ones waiting to be discovered. Other herbal products include herbal wreaths, potpourris and herbal tea blends.

If your objective is self-sufficiency, you should try to structure your herb garden and herbal products so that you have a continual supply of these necessities in times of shortage.

Recommended Reading

American Medicinal Plants: An Illustrated and Descriptive Guide to Plants Indigenous to and Naturalized in the United States Which Are Used in Medicine by Charles F. Millspaugh, Dover Publications, Inc., 1974. ISBN 0-486-23034-1. Although this is an unabridged replication of the 1892 edition, its 804 pages are filled with information on 180 individual plants and their medicinal uses.

Rodale's Illustrated Encyclopedia of Herbs, edited by Claire Kowalchik and William H. Hylton. Rodale Press Inc., 1987. ISBN 0-87857-898-6. With more than half a million copies in print, this encyclopedia lists over 150 herbs alphabetically. It is a good introductory book for growing herbs, and contains a wide spectrum of herb uses in its 552 pages.

The Healing Herbs: The Ultimate Guide to the Curative Power of Nature's Medicines by Michael Castleman. Rodale Press Inc., 1991. ISBN 0-87857-934-6. This book contains herb remedies for over 200 conditions and diseases.

The Encyclopedia of Herbs, Spices & Flavorings: A Cook's Compendium by Elisabeth Lambert Ortiz. Dorling Kindersley, Inc., 1992. ISBN 1-56458-065-2. A colorful (750 photographs) and descriptive book of herbs and spices with a heavy focus on cooking and preserving.

A Modern Herbal: The Medicinal, Culinary, Cosmetic and Economic Properties, Cultivation and Folk-Lore of Herbs, Grasses, Fungi, Shrubs and Trees with Their Modern Scientific Uses by Mrs. M. Grieve. (two volume set) Dover Publications, Inc., 1982. ISBN 0-486-22798-7, 0-486-22799-5. An unabridged reproduction of the original 1931 edition, this two-book set is loaded with information on herbal uses.

Jude's Herbal Home Remedies: Natural Health, Beauty & Home-Care Secrets by Jude C. Williams, Llewellyn Publications, 1992. ISBN 0-87542-8699-X. A treasure house full of common products that you can make yourself, using material from your own garden.

Chapter Six

Growing Non-Food And Other Valuable Crops

When you are considering growing crops to increase your security and financial independence, you should be aware that in no way are you limited to growing only crops that produce food. Furthermore, many crops fall into the category of being multi-purpose, and offer extra opportunities to the grower.

Bees are a source of honey plus they will pollinate your crops.
(Martin P. Waterman photo.)

In addition to valuable crops that have no food value, there are also some food crops that have other uses besides their value as sustenance. For instance, corn and grains can be grown to make alcohol, and certain vines can be grown to make baskets and furniture.

There are many examples of non-food crops, and many are overlooked and disregarded. This does not mean that their value is diminished to the self-sufficiency gardener. Many books about native tribes

of North America and the immigrants who settled here detail how so much of the native plant material was used for fuel, shelter, clothing, tools and other necessities of life. Some of the non-food uses are detailed below.

The Woodlot

If you do your homework, there could be money in growing trees for resale to the nursery trade or as living or cut Christmas trees.
(Martin P. Waterman photo.)

A prime example of a non-food use of plant material is that of a woodlot. A well-managed woodlot can heat your home forever and provide you with enough fuel for cooking and other uses. Although uncommon, a wood fired generator is worthy of consideration for those with no shortage of firewood, yet with a need for emergency or everyday electrical current.

You may also be able to cut enough extra lumber each year to be able to sell the excess for a profit, or build anything from furniture and crafts to homes and other structures. You can even make many of your own tools from the wood that you find on your property.

The money you earn from a woodlot, or a property with lumber, can pay the taxes on the property or help finance other property you are trying to purchase. This is a good manner in which to accumulate and hold land. I know of several lumbermen who purchased farms with stands of timber growing on the property. The money they earned from cutting and selling the lumber on the land often came close to equaling the amount they paid for the farm. In a few cases, it even exceeded the cost. The wood does not even have to be sold to a lumber mill. There is often a ready market for fence posts, firewood and even the sawdust and chips from your cutting and clearing activities. You can usually learn about this market from checking the classified ads in your local newspaper.

Some entrepreneurs will purchase a stand of trees and bring a portable sawmill to the woodlot in order to cut lumber for their own use or produce lumber they can sell. If you have checked the cost of lumber lately, you can see that there are profits for efficient operators. In fact, many people earn a very good living buying small timber stands or contracting to cut on someone else's land in order to produce high-quality lumber. Since the forest products industry is heavily unionized, from the people who cut the trees to the truck drivers and the sawmill workers, by the time it goes through a wholesaler and to your local lumber yard, the prices can be so steep as to be ridiculous.

In my area, there are even some small boat builders who produce all the lumber they need from their own woodlots. They have complete control over the lumber, from thinning and cutting to creating the finished product. Naturally, they can beat their competition, since their costs are dramatically reduced, and they can also create specialty and custom products which are always in demand.

If your land has a pond or you intend to build a pond, you could stock it with trout or catfish such as these for year-round recreation and food.
(U.S.D.A. photo.)

It is a good idea to know who is doing any lumbering in your area. Often, a piece of land that has just been lumbered can be picked up at a very reasonable price. Also, many government agencies and organizations will provide free seedlings to replant a deforested area. Of course, these seedlings will take decades to grow, but in the meantime you can thin the woodlot of its hardwood for firewood and count on the new stand as security for later in life or for your retirement.

If you own a piece of land or have an option on a piece of land and do not want to lumber it yourself, contact people who lumber and see the price they will pay in order to lumber on your land. If you do enter into a contract with someone to lumber your land, keep the contract time as short as possible. That way you do not have to renew if you are not pleased with the job being done or the payment process. In addition, shorter contracts force the lumberman to work quickly. Many people who lumber land will tie up several pieces so that they will have a steady supply of income for years, while preventing their competition from getting the land.

*These maple trees have had taps inserted
so that the maple sap can be collected
and made into maple syrup.*
(Martin P. Waterman photo.)

It is not hard to find land that has not been lumbered. Many people do not like the idea of lumbering land, since the equipment and loss of lumber can do temporary damage to the environment. Some people will not sell the lumber off their land for any price. However, they will often sell their land to someone else whom they think will be involved with the property for a long time, and not acquiring it just for a quick buck. This is especially so of those owners who have a very strong emotional attachment to their land.

There are many books on how to properly manage a woodlot, and if you follow some of the principles they outline, you can grow a self-sustaining stand of lumber and other useful plants that will continue to support you and the native wildlife for years to come.

Housing

Many people, especially those in the back-to-the-land movement, will purchase land so that they can build a home on it from the trees on the property. If this is your objective, make sure that you still have

the type of wood you require remaining on the property. Certain trees such as cedar are slow-growing, so just because there are many cedar seedlings does not mean that you will be building that log cabin in the near future.

Housing does not need to be complex, and you can easily build a survival shelter, depending on complexity, in a number of hours. The option is yours, but depending on the amount of land you have and the type of lumber you are growing, you will have more alternatives.

Craft Items

Craft supplies and finished craftworks can provide an income, especially if you are in a tourism area. Growing your own craft supplies to use or sell is easier than you may have imagined.

More and more people are discovering the pleasure and sense of accomplishment that can be obtained from making their own craftworks. There is something about a piece of art, a gift or anything that is homemade that makes it extra special.

Many different types of material that can help you practice crafts can be grown in your very own garden. This can make your creations unique, since not only are you creating them with your own love and imagination, but you are also helping to create them with materials that you have sown, grown, harvested and prepared in your garden.

*It never ceases to amaze me the number of products
that can be made from the work of bees.*
(Honey Tree Farm photo.)

The number of craft items that can be grown in your garden or harvested from nature can be mind-boggling, especially once you understand the many ways in which you can use them.

The following are but a few examples of how craft items can be grown in your garden.

Dried Flowers

Dried flowers are commonly used in craftmaking. They can be used to decorate wreaths, baskets or other items, and can be fashioned into eye appealing dry flower arrangements. The best way to preserve flowers is by air-drying. Certain flowers do better than others, but in general, most flowers air-dry very well.

The best flowers to use are ones that have not yet fully opened, since drying will cause them to open more.

You may have to remove many of the leaves from the stems, since they will interfere with the air circulation needed to dry them.

You will want to dry the flowers as soon as possible after picking so that they will retain their colors better and not have any chance to rot.

The flowers should be placed in a dark warm place that is also dry. Darkness is important, since light will bleach out the colors. An ideal place for this might be an attic or a closet that receives adequate air circulation.

The flowers should be put in small bunches. They can be held together with an elastic band or string and then hung upside down on a string. The heads should not be too close to each other, and the bunches should have enough space so that there is room for the air to circulate around them and remove the moisture. Certain plants such as ornamental grasses and Chinese lanterns must be dried right side up in order for them to retain their desirable shapes.

Baskets & Wreaths

English ivy, wisteria and grape vines can be used to make baskets and wreaths. For baskets alone, you can use branches and twigs from willows, elders, elms and other trees as well as grasses, cattails, day lilies, reeds and even strips of bark. There are many excellent books available on basket- and wreath-making. These items, of course, can be decorated with the dried flowers described earlier, as well as other items such as pine cones and other decorative objects.

Cornhusks

Cornhusks can be used to make many craft items. One of the most popular uses is to make corn-husk dolls. Cornhusks that have been allowed to dry on the stem are usually much better than those picked green and then dried. However, both types have been used successfully to make a number of craft items. Cornhusk dolls are made using string, thread, pipe cleaners and glue. The silk from the ears can also be saved and used as hair.

Nature has always been used as a source for art and craft materials. This practice is having a resurgence, as more and more people have a greater appreciation for nature and our environment. For instance, many people are now growing or collecting material such as alders, burdock, cranberry and goldenrod in order to make their own natural dyes.

Once you understand the basic principles of craft-making, you will discover that your garden and Mother Nature are unlimited sources of material and ideas with which to work. In fact, nature's own textures, colors and tapestries are often the inspiration for making craftworks and capturing the essence of nature, together with its beauty, so as to reflect it in our homes.

Grow Your Own Alcohol

Another valuable commodity that you can grow is corn to produce your own alcohol. If you waited in any long gasoline lineups at the service station during the oil embargo of the early 1970s, you will have an understanding of how important fuel for your automobile really is to your functioning and ultimate survival.

There are many excellent books on how to make your own fuel for your transportation and other machinery needs.

Your Own Happy Hunting Grounds

Some landowners purchase land with the objective of establishing an ideal habitat for wildlife. For instance, deer love apple trees and other types of foliage. This gives the landowner a place where he is able to hunt for his own food. Some landowners go a step further and become guides or rent their backwoods home as a hunting camp or a getaway.

Whether or not you decide to turn your property into a hunting camp, the fact of the matter is that in times of emergency, you have already developed your own area that is available for hunting fresh game or catching fish. In fact, by clearing certain areas and planting certain types of vegetation, you can make sure that your area is a favorite habitat for various forms of wildlife. You can even build a pond and stock it with trout or other species for year-round recreation or food. The possibilities are really unlimited when you take the time to do the research and are careful not to try to grow too quickly.

One of the advantages of trading up to rural gardening from urban gardening is that there is an abundance of wildlife.
(U.S.D.A. photo.)

Feed for Livestock

So you're not a vegetarian, and all the fruit and vegetables you can grow are impressive... but what about meat? You can actually raise your own meat! Let me explain. You can grow your own feed, and this can support a cow, chickens, hogs or just about any type of livestock. In fact, if you are able to grow abundant food, you can use your culls or byproducts to feed the animals. For example, cull potatoes make excellent cattle feed. After your garden is harvested, the remaining plant material can also be used as feed.

If you do not want livestock, you may be able to sell the hay on your land to a local farmer. There never seems to be enough hay around for feed for livestock. The prices will be different depending on whether you cut it or allow someone else to do it. Check the prices in your area, since hay prices can vary dramatically. You may even find that your neighbor's land has hay, and you may be able to purchase or trade goods for the use of this pasture.

Many land holders are looking towards exotic livestock for income and security. Elk are just one of the animals that are being raised domestically.
(Martin P. Waterman photo.)

If your land has some clear areas, you may be able to support lambs or cattle. If this is the case, try to choose breeds which are not prone to sickness. Many breeds, particularly historic ones, can be hardy and quite self-sufficient. Again, the idea is that these animals should be helping to support you and not the other way around. There is a trade-off inasmuch as many newer breeds are fast-growing and large producers of meat and dairy products. However, if the veterinarian has to come out once or twice a month, you are not really achieving your goal of being self-sufficient.

Your garden can help support livestock such as pigs.
(Martin P. Waterman photo.)

If you do have cattle or goats, you will be able to have your own milk and dairy products. As you are probably aware, certain products such as cheeses can be very expensive. There is no need for you to go without these delicacies. Many firms manufacture milk pasteurizers, butter churners and other equipment with the small farmer in mind.

There are many types of livestock and fowl that you may consider raising. For instance, quail do not take much room and are an ideal entry into raising birds for food. From that point you may want to try chickens, pheasants or turkeys. Remember, your objective is not to compete with large processors or your local grocery store — it is to provide yourself with a safe and secure supply of healthy and nutritious food, come Hell or high water.

Recommended Reading

Natural Baskets: Create Over 20 Unique Baskets with Material Gathered in Gardens, Fields, and Woods edited by Maryanne Gillooly, Storey Communications, Inc., 1992. ISBN 0-88266-793-9. Seven basketmakers teach different methods. In some areas, natural baskets can command good prices.

Country Fresh Gifts: Recipes and Projects for Your Garden and Country Kitchen by the editors of Storey Publishing, Storey Communications, Inc., 1991, ISBN 0-88266-660-6. Over 200 recipes and projects, including soaps, candles, potpourris, dried flowers and, of course, all kinds of foods and preserves.

Forget the Gas Pumps — Make your Own Fuel by Jim Wortham and Barbara Whitener. Marathon International Book Company, 1991. ISBN 0-915216-43-3. This book tells you how to obtain a permit to operate an alcohol still, as well as providing the easy step-by-step directions on how to convert your car so it will be able to run on the alcohol mixture.

Chapter Seven

Edible Landscaping

Edible landscaping is the practice of using landscape plants for food as well as for other purposes, including their aesthetic beauty. The process of landscaping a property by itself may have many benefits, both financial and otherwise.

A property that is properly landscaped can result in lower energy bills by providing shade and moderating the wind. A properly designed landscape can also guarantee you a degree of privacy in a manner that is very natural and not likely to draw attention.

Money spent on landscaping will usually add much more equity to a property than fixing up the interior or exterior of a home.
(Martin P. Waterman photo.)

Real estate agents know the value of a properly landscaped property. One of the most important benefits of landscaping your property is that a property which has been landscaped can easily add from 10-20% to the purchase price of a home when it is sold. The percentage range is even higher if one believes the quotes from various real estate agencies. If you have a home that is valued at $100,000 and you have increased its value a minimum of 15% by creating an attractive landscape, you have in effect created an additional $15,000 in equity. Suppose you spent $3,000 on plants and materials. This still leaves you with $12,000 of equity, which is more than some people earn in a year.

Add to this value the fact that for every landscape plant, be it a vine, a specimen tree or a bush, a hedge or even a ground cover, there is a substitute that will produce some kind of fruit or nut. Also, keep in mind that it is not difficult to produce thousands of pounds of fruit (and many dollars) from an average sized urban lot. With careful planning, these edible landscape plants can be selected so that the ripening and harvesting are spread throughout the season.

Many fruit trees like cherries and peaches are very ornamental when they bloom. There is now a new generation of dwarf cultivars which can give you a wide selection in a limited amount of space. The possibilities are endless, and once you become familiar with the items you can grow in your area, you will probably be astounded by the variety of food and the yields that can be expected on even the smallest lots.

Unfortunately, edible landscaping is misunderstood and, much under utilized. The term "edible landscaping" is a fairly recent buzzword for the age-old practice of using landscape plants for their value as a food source as well as for their beauty. In frontier times and times of economic woes, edible landscaping was cultivated almost automatically as a matter of necessity and survival, or at the very least as a source of supplementing scarce resources. Fruits, nuts and berries are most often used in edible landscaping, although vegetables, grains and root crops can also be used.

Today, edible landscaping has been making a vibrant comeback. This is for a number of practical reasons. Gardening has become a very popular pastime once again, and statistics show that there are 70 million households in the United States in which at least one family member is a gardener. In addition, with all of the environmental concern about losing the world's rain forests and fears over pesticide use and abuse, the gardening movement is winning new converts. Many large environmental groups such as Global Relief have emerged, and they are encouraging the planting of trees and vegetation.

Even though most people feel the greatest benefits of edible landscaping are growing your own tasty food without the fear of pesticides and the feeling of security that producing your own food brings, an obvious advantage is often overlooked. Even an average sized urban lot can provide several thousand dollars worth of fresh produce if managed properly. Therefore, it is important to know the type of yields to expect from various plants, and how long it will take them to start producing fruit. With a pencil and paper and some good library books, you can sketch out your property with various types of edible landscape designs and calculate what the potential yields may be.

What To Grow

This consideration is not as difficult as it may seem. There are so many varieties of food that can be used in an edible landscape that you can let your taste buds be your guide. The only other considerations are how much maintenance you want to devote to your planting and what varieties lend themselves best to the kind of preserving and storage methods you prefer. For instance, if you like jams, fruit would be important. If you want to grow easy items to preserve, such as nuts, then you should investigate nut trees.

It is important to be aware that there is an explosion of new varieties being developed by breeders. In addition, older varieties are being rediscovered, usually because they lend themselves to

organic growing practices. Add to this the new varieties being imported from Asia and the former Soviet Union, and you can see that the selections are almost limitless. The changes in certain varieties achieved by breeding programs make edible landscaping all that much easier.

You may want to consider colors and textures in addition to size. Landscaping can serve many purposes. You can grow edible landscape plants that will have fragrant flowers. Other types of landscapes can be designed to attract birds or butterflies. Some prefer Japanese-style gardens, while others like a tropical or subtropical look. One of the most popular themes is to give your landscape a natural woods-edge look. It is best to investigate all the possibilities. As you look at various types of food that you can use in a landscape, you will be assembling a palette of textures, shapes and colors with which to construct your own individual landscape.

One of the most popular trends in landscaping today is a water garden. What better way to guarantee yourself some water for irrigation in times of drought while enhancing the value and productivity of your garden?

There are hundreds of excellent books on landscaping. In addition, there are also some fine instructional video tapes that are now available. They underscore the fact that the trick to successful edible landscaping is substituting existing traditional ornamental plants with plants that can provide you with food.

There is a fruit plant for any landscaping addition that you may be contemplating. Landscape practices are relatively simple and tend to gravitate to traditional designs, and this has not changed much over the years.

Your own landscape needs will depend on your site. Most landscapes consist of single specimen plantings, large shade trees, foundation planting, rock gardens, hedges and areas for climbing vines. Besides staying with a traditional landscape, you can also deviate with different patterns and arrangements. For instance, in my backyard I have a 60´ x 60´ vineyard in Zone 4b. It provides an estate-like focal point in the garden which I overlook from the second floor where I often spend time writing. It also gives an interesting space so that I can walk up and down the vineyard rows. More importantly, the "minivineyard" provides over 1,000 pounds of grapes (or half a ton) which I use for juice, fresh eating and preserves.

Many may not have this type of room on their lot, but the principle remains the same, whether you want a small apple or citrus orchard, or prefer nuts and berries or any other combination.

Landscaping can also provide income for those who want to sell and install some of the plants they grow or purchase from other growers and wholesalers.
(Martin P. Waterman photo.)

For a summer windbreak I have a row of hardy plums, and I also use gooseberries, currants and elderberries as hedging material.

For a simple understanding of this concept, just think of landscaping as shade trees, hedges and vines. For each of these three categories, there are some excellent choices.

Favorite Choices

I have some favorite choices, depending on the climate, which incidentally have also become very popular among fruit growing fans. In many instances, some people start growing fruit as a hobby, and in their quest to try more and more new varieties find themselves edible landscaping in their quest to use every last inch of available property.

For many, the best thing about growing your own food is that it tastes nothing like the produce you buy at your local grocery store. It is a shame that so many have never tasted a tree ripened apricot, peach or plum. The produce in the supermarket is usually not selected primarily on the basis of taste. It is selected so that it can take the pounding of shipping and handling, so it often seems to have skin like leather. It is almost always picked when unripe, so that it will keep longer. A friend of mine said it best when he bought some plums at the supermarket and then remarked that he might as well eat the cellophane they were wrapped in because he couldn't tell the difference in the texture. Fruit will usually ripen after harvesting (grapes are one exception), but will never reach the high sugar, vitamin and flavor content of a tree- or bush ripened fruit.

I will use five of my favorite fruits as examples of ideal landscape plants and their best uses.

Do not neglect a popular fruit such as the apple. Apples can be made into juice and sauce, or can be dried, canned or stored. It is always good to grow some of the varieties that are listed as excellent "keepers," which will store for several months. Apples have been used in the formal landscape for centuries, and through pruning can fit into several landscape applications, from hedging and specimen planting to being large shade trees.

No matter where you practice edible landscaping, there is a multitude of plant materials from which to choose, such as these bananas growing in Florida.
(Martin P. Waterman photo.)

In the warmer areas of the United States into Zone 9 and 10, bananas have to be one of the most spectacular of landscape plants. One of the tricks of growing bananas is that they will not tolerate winds.

This can make them ideal for the home landscape where they can be sheltered by a fence or a building. In the United States, bananas are not subject to pest problems. Bananas are very productive. In fact, banana plantations average between 10 to 25 tons of fruit per acre. One banana plant can yield 100 pounds of fruit after it matures in slightly over a year. There are many varieties, and almost all surpass supermarket purchased bananas in flavor and texture. Bananas are now in vogue, and there are currently many nurseries handling these items.

Citrus fruits are also under utilized landscape plants. They can even be trained as hedge plants, and do yield themselves to shaping. One of the greatest things about citrus is the variety available, which is continually expanding. Some of the newer hybrids and varieties from Asia are opening up new areas where some citrus can be grown. There are actually some growers who are growing citrus in Oregon.

My favorite landscape plant is the grape. It can be grown in every state, and the uses are wide ranging, from wine to gourmet recipes. Grapes will soon turn a chain-link fence into an privacy hedge. It will turn an arbor into a subtropical looking shade area. Short trellises can be used as dividers in the garden or back yard to divide spaces. Grapes can also yield between four to ten tons per acre. That is why wine in some areas sells for less than milk or orange juice.

For hedging, I like currants, gooseberries, elderberries or Nanking cherries. A single mature currant or gooseberry bush will provide six to ten pounds of fruit. Multiply this by 10, 20 or 30 bushes for a hedge, and you are talking about as much as 180 to 300 lbs. Currants come in red, white and black, and make tasty preserves. The white currants, which are making a comeback, are the best for fresh eating, although all varieties are tasty. A gooseberry bush not only has an attractive appearance, but at harvest time can provide the ingredients necessary for gooseberry pie and other desserts.

Nanking cherries are an excellent choice for the North. The fruit makes excellent juice and jelly, and is also good to eat fresh. The Nanking cherry bush has velvety foliage, and has the added advantage of pretty pink flowers when it blooms in the spring.

Elderberries are an interesting plant and very well-suited to the North. There are many varieties that are available. They are another versatile fruit that can be used for juice, wine making, jams and pies.

Another fruit which is high-yielding and can be grown in almost every state is the kiwi. Most think of this as a tropical fruit, but there are varieties hardy into U.S.D.A. Zone 3. More kiwi varieties are being released, and new ones are continually being developed. The kiwi is becoming more and more popular, especially because of its high nutritional value. The kiwi's best uses are in the same applications where grapes would be used, since they have similar growth habits.

Nuts are another high-yielding food source. The nuts often take little preparation for long-term storage. However, some nut trees are unpredictable and may not bear annually. Some trees may also take years to begin production. Therefore, it is important to have a variety of different edible landscape plants. This will provide you with insurance, since it is very unlikely that all your varieties will fall victim to diseases or pests.

Of course, certain varieties of fruit are better suited for some landscape applications than others. Plums have a useful place in the landscape, and when they burst out in a profusion of white flowers in the spring, they are very attractive. Some plum trees are very ornamental, such as Patterson's Pride. The growth habit of the tree is an attractive weeping shape. The fruit is of high quality, and the tree is extremely hardy.

Some gardeners who follow the principle of edible landscaping try to plan their varieties so that they have a selection of fruit from late spring until fall, as well as an extra supply to store for winter. This can easily be achieved by considering the ripening times of the various fruits before you plant. Certain fruits such as apples enable you to pick varieties that will ripen from mid-August to early October.

Edible landscaping is not just for fruit. Herbs and certain vegetables can be a welcome addition to your flower garden or to your general landscape plans. Perennial herbs such as chives and tarragon have been used as attractive additions to the landscape, and there are many others you may wish to consider, depending on your tastes.

You may want to consider adding medicinal plants to your landscape, and there is also your interior environment. The inside of a house or apartment is usually neglected when it comes to growing food and medicine. New varieties and hydroponics are making indoor growing a fast-growing trend. It is important to note that gardeners in cooler climates have been growing tender fruit varieties in containers that can be taken indoors for the winter.

One of the best features about edible landscaping is that you can grow varieties that you will probably never see in a grocery store. Many of the plants, such as raspberries and blackberries, are so perishable that they are rarely available in the stores, and if they are, it is for such a short time, and the prices are usually exorbitant. You can grow an almost endless list of uncommon fruit such as paw paws, Saskatoon berries, quince, figs, guava, blueberries, and, if you are really daring, you can experiment with other little known fruits such as rose hips, which are rich in vitamins and flavor and have a number of culinary uses. Roses, of course, are one of the most useful plants in the landscape.

There are other benefits to landscaping. It increases property values and adds to the beauty of the neighborhood. Doctors and therapists are also recognizing the health benefits, particularly for the elderly, of activities associated with the garden. Using edible landscaping is another way of employing this often neglected resource to further enrich your security, while keeping others unaware that you are practicing self-sufficiency gardening.

Best zones for some of the better known edible landscape fruit, nut & berry varieties:

Apples	4 – 9
Apricots	4 – 9
Avocados	9 – 10
Banana	9 – 10
Citrus	8 – 10
Currants	2 – 6
Figs	6 – 9
Grapes	3 – 10
Hazelnuts	4 – 8
Kiwi	3 – 10
Mango	10
Macadamia	8 – 10
Papaya	10
Passion Fruit	10
Pistachio	7 – 10
Peaches	5 – 9
Pears	4 – 9
Pecans	6 – 10

Persimmons	6 – 10
Plums	3 – 8
Pomegranates	8 – 9
Strawberries	2 – 10
Walnuts	3 – 9

Recommended Reading

Designing and Maintaining Your Edible Landscape Naturally by Robert Kourick. Metamorphic Press, 1986. ISBN 0-9615848-0-7. *Mother Earth News* said that this book "could be the most comprehensive guide in existence to growing vegetables, fruits, flowers and herbs for both ornamental and culinary purposes." I heartily agree.

Chapter Eight

Greenhouse Gardening

Many growers find that after they get established, they want to push their gardening to the limits by utilizing greenhouses, hydroponics and other methods to reach their food self-sufficiency objectives. In many cases, these methods can be used to make up for shortfalls in nature. For instance, a greenhouse will prolong the growing season in a northern or high altitude location, while an indoor hydroponic system can provide fresh food year-round and at times when certain naturally grown produce is unavailable.

By attaching a sunroom to your home, you can have the advantages of a greenhouse plus energy savings.
(Martin P. Waterman photo.)

One of the most exciting aspects of greenhouse and hydroponic growing is that the prices for many systems are coming down. Also, once you have a basic understanding of how these systems work, you can usually construct your own, often with simple and easily procured materials.

Choosing a Greenhouse

It is hard to plan your first greenhouse correctly, since it is so difficult to predict all the kinds of plants you may want to grow in your new greenhouse. Making an accurate assessment of the total greenhouse size that is needed often is more easily said than done. I have learned through experience that most gardeners will quickly outgrow their first greenhouse, and will soon realize that it may be inadequate. Once they discover that there are so many additional crops and uses that are suited to their greenhouse, their original plans may become obsolete quickly.

I am not going to go into detail on the technical requirements of certain types of greenhouse plants. There is ample information readily available on these topics. However, I have tried to compile a list that outlines about a dozen factors that you should consider before you procure your first greenhouse.

What to Grow

This may not sound like an important question but believe me, it is. I thought I knew exactly what I would do the second I had my new greenhouse. Was I ever wrong! Greenhouses open up more possibilities than you can imagine, so it is good to start to plan as if you already have one.

I had originally wanted my greenhouse so that I could propagate material such as grape vines and fruit trees in the spring, and also start seeds for experimental varieties that I wanted to try growing. Of course, when I realized I could start vegetable plants in the spring, have an early crop of peppers and tomatoes and have late season strawberries into November, I became painfully aware that I had not truly taken the time to consider many of the options that would open up to me once I had my greenhouse. I find that I am doing many additional things with the greenhouse beyond what I thought would be possible. I am starting tropical house plants, and growing bananas and citrus which are moved indoors in the fall.

Therefore, when you are contemplating buying or building your greenhouse, take some time and think about all the varieties you want to grow. Then, take some more time to think about the varieties that you may want to grow in the future. Better still, buy or borrow a book on greenhouse growing and study all the possibilities. I was surprised how many books have been written on greenhouse growing, and I found that our local library had a very impressive selection, since this is such a popular topic. When you are contemplating what you may want to grow, it is a good idea to discuss it with your spouse and loved ones to factor in their favorite foods. When you have a better conception of the things you will be growing, your questions will begin to be answered, and you should begin to get a better idea of the type of capacity you may need. I still find myself considering new crops almost every week. This is another benefit of owning a greenhouse. You get to scheme about and experiment with new varieties that you could never grow previously.

When to Grow

The amount of time that you will be using your greenhouse is also an important fact to consider. If you plan to use it regularly and it becomes your entertainment, recreation and even therapy, you will want a structure that you can use as much as possible. How much time you spend in your greenhouse is also very important. Some people will use their greenhouse only in the spring. They find that by growing their own landscape bedding plants and starting vegetable transplants early, they can save as much as several hundred dollars a year, especially if

they have a big lot. Others like to move their house plants into the greenhouse in the summer or grow an early crop of vegetables. Still others like to grow a late fall crop as well. Obviously, the more you use your greenhouse, the more you may want to invest in it to make sure it is comfortable to work in and able to accommodate all the growing time you want to donate.

Measuring only 8 by 12 feet, this plastic covered wood greenhouse produces new plants and food from early spring until late autumn.
(Martin P. Waterman photo.)

Of course, if you use your greenhouse in the early spring and late fall, you may need heat and artificial lighting. You will also have to consider whether or not you want a double layer of plastic, which insulates better than a single layer by trapping warm air. You may also want to consider double-paned glass. If you use your greenhouse in the summer, you may also need some type of cooling system.

How Big is Big Enough?

This is a very important consideration. I outgrew my greenhouse in the span of a few days. It was a little embarrassing, to say the least.

One item you may wish to consider is the expandability of the greenhouse you intend to purchase or build. Many greenhouse kits are expandable, and sections can be continually added. The ability to do this so that your structure can be expanded is a very good feature. However, be careful that the expansion of your greenhouse does not become more expensive than if you just built or purchased a second structure.

"Big" can mean many things to different people. Do you want it big enough so that you can have good-sized work benches? This is important if you do not like to bend, because if your plants are on the ground, you will be doing a lot of bending.

A greenhouse that is too small may not have room for an aisle down the center. Take some time to think about how wide you want your aisle to be, or, if you are installing benches, how much room they will take up. A greenhouse should have an aisle wide enough to allow you easy access to all the plant material.

Do you want to put in a heat retention system such as water-filled jars or drums? These will take up room, and must be factored into your plans. Do you want room for a hammock, or perhaps a chair? A greenhouse is an excellent place to relax, read, converse with friends, meditate, snooze and even hide.

The first greenhouse I built was much too small. This led me to the discovery of a formula. The volume of an empty greenhouse will always become full, since the amount of material you will want to grow will always be equal to or greater than the available space. Height is also an important consideration. If you are growing vines in the greenhouse, you may want a high ceiling.

If you like the idea of hanging plants, you may also want a high ceiling so that the pots and the plants are not in your face. In addition, you will require a structure that can support this type of weight. Some types of hanging plants, in addition to increasing your yields, will also provide some degree of shading, which can be beneficial on hot summer days.

Climatic Considerations

This is often ignored by many growers, but it is important. If you live in an area where you have considerable snow in the winter, you will want a structure that will not collapse. If your area has a history of hailstorms, this could also have a bearing on the type of greenhouse and covering you buy or build. Do you live in an area with high winds? If this is the case, you may have to consider anchoring your greenhouse, or else you may have to retrieve it from the next county after a wind storm has ended. I anchored my greenhouse by driving wooden stakes about three feet into the ground around the frame, and then nailing the stakes to the wooden base. So far, even on a very windy day, the greenhouse does not budge, even when the doors are closed.

The prevalent wind direction in your area will also tell you how to position your structure. For instance, my structure does not have a cooling system. It is not necessary, since I live in a cool maritime climate with a short season. Therefore, I positioned the greenhouse so that the constant east-west breeze will blow through it when both doors are opened. This keeps the greenhouse cool in the summer. It is not an elaborate cooling system, but for my purposes it works very well.

Aesthetics

Some will argue that aesthetics is secondary to function in a greenhouse. I would not normally bring up the question of how your greenhouse looks, except for three facts. The first is that you do not want a greenhouse that after two or three years of use will look like a shanty greenhouse. Secondly, for those in urban areas, you don't want something that will upset the neighbors or authorities. Having a greenhouse is a status item, and status often brings jealousy in our society. Some greenhouses that you can buy look so shoddy that I would be embarrassed to own one.

In addition, many municipalities have become so petty that they require a building permit for anything larger than, and even including, a doghouse. This is something to be aware of in your planning stage. My greenhouse is, to my sensibility, very good looking, and I am very proud of it.

Materials

Should you choose glass, plastic or fiberglass coverings? There are good and bad arguments for all these materials, and entire book chapters have been devoted to debating this; the result has been many different conclusions. I chose plastic for several reasons. First of all, the price advantage was dramatic. Secondly, I thought that it was the best-constructed greenhouse at the price I wanted. I also decided that if I liked it, I would then buy another one. My next greenhouse will also be plastic and the same style, because I would rather invest the differential in buying a larger greenhouse and plant materials it.

Should the frame be made of steel, aluminum, plastic or wood? Again, there is much debate about this. You will have to decide what your needs and budget are and choose appropriately. Incidentally, my greenhouse has a wood frame which I like very much. The wood is soaked in paint during the manufacturing process, and lasts a very long time.

To Build or Buy

Originally, I was going to build a greenhouse. I love building things. I have been collecting glass windows from yard sales for years. However, whenever I sat down to draw up plans, I found that building my own greenhouse would probably be more expensive than buying a greenhouse kit. If you are considering building a greenhouse, make certain that your materials list is very thorough, because the project could nickel-and-dime you to death. Do not forget incidentals such as hardware, sealant and paint, which can add up to quite a bit of money.

If you are building from a kit, as I did for my greenhouse, make sure that the instructions are easy to follow and that you need a minimum number of hand tools and do not require a degree in engineering from MIT to assemble it.

Cold frames are inexpensive to make and can help you extend your growing season and start your own transplants and nursery materials.
(Martin P. Waterman photo.)

Incidentally, I did find a great use for all those windows that I purchased at yard sales. I built cold frames, and I use these to start bedding plants and grow an early supply of lettuce, usually when there is still snow on the ground.

Of course, you can always add a greenhouse to your existing house. By doing this, you can benefit by adding equity to your home. The solar heating provided by a well-designed greenhouse can bring you impressive savings. A proper greenhouse addition can lower heating bills to the extent that the addition can be paid for in just a few years. There are many excellent books on this topic for those who want to investigate this type of greenhouse.

Self-Sufficiency vs. Commercial Greenhouse Uses

Let's say you start several dozen tomato plants for your own use in January, move them into the greenhouse in March, and in May have a hundred pounds or so more than you can use. You talk to your local produce manager, convenience store owner or restaurant, and find that they will buy all the fresh tomatoes you can supply. This may sound unusual, but it is exactly how many greenhouse growers earn money to supplement their hobby and often go on to become successful commercial growers. The types of commercial growing are endless: fresh herbs, cut flowers, rose bushes, fruit trees, bonsai specimens, fruits, vegetables, landscape and ornamental plants. You will also have the advantage of specializing in varieties that are ideal for your market. This alone can give you an advantage over some of the large factory-style propagators. Recently, I visited a local garden center. I know the owner, and he told me that they could not propagate certain plants fast enough to meet demand, even though they have acres upon acres of greenhouses. I learned that they were constantly looking for contract growers who could help supply them with big sellers such as citrosa (mosquito repellent plant), geraniums, clematis and several other different varieties of herbs and flowers. Commercial considerations may be the farthest thought from your mind, but when neighbors and others begin to come and offer you money for tomatoes or plants, the temptation to sell a few and grow a few more may be too hard to resist. In fact, it may be downright profitable.

The Foundation of Your Greenhouse

What are you going to use as a foundation for your greenhouse? If you have a concrete pad, this is great. It will help store heat during the day and release it at night in the cooler times of the year, and can prolong your growing season. You could put your greenhouse on some turf, but if it is a wooden structure the base can begin to rot after a few years. You may want to look into buying a greenhouse that uses pressure-treated lumber for the wood in its base, or which has a plastic or aluminum base. There are many alternatives to an expensive concrete pad or concrete footings. You can create a pad from leveled gravel which will allow water drainage and prevent rot. You could put down some of those concrete patio squares that are often used for paths and walkways. In any event, you will have the type of foundation you need. To prevent the cost from exceeding your budget, be sure to do an investigation of different foundation materials. I found out by accident that it is important not to have any spaces between the pad and your greenhouse. One chilly spring night, cold air leaked in through a small crack between the concrete pad and the base of the greenhouse. It froze a few leaves on nearby plants. I remedied this by filling the crack with a handful of sandy soil.

To Heat or Not to Heat

This is another big question. I had not intended to heat my greenhouse. Now, in order to extend the season, I have changed my mind. Heating can be done in so many different ways and through such various systems that you need to consider how long you want to prolong your method. At a certain point, the cost of heating may diminish the value of any crop you are growing. Then again, the thought of having green plants and fresh nutritious vegetables into winter may offset the power costs. Therefore, it is important to look at these factors as well. A greenhouse structure, if built onto an existing house, can provide heat via solar radiation in the day, and be closed off at night when it will not be in jeopardy of freezing. With freestanding greenhouses, there are some simple ways to prolong the season, especially if you are just trying to add a few weeks. In my area, the first fall frost can occur as early as September. A local hobby greenhouse grower heats his greenhouse on those nights when there are frost warnings. He uses three brooding lights that are normally employed for raising chicks, and they provide enough heat to prevent freezing temperatures in his greenhouse well into November. Other growers will buy electric heaters and set the thermostat so that the heat will come on when temperatures approach freezing. Still others have small wood stoves which they start before bed, and this keeps their greenhouses toasty warm all night.

Electrical Requirements

You may not think that you have any electrical requirements but you may need more than you know. Of course, you will have to consider how your plants will fare if they are dependent upon electricity for watering, heating or cooling, and this supply is interrupted.

If you add an electric misting, lighting, heating or cooling system, or a good sound system to keep the plants growing, you may have to consider at least adding an outdoor outlet so that you can run an extension cord through the greenhouse. An outdoor outlet is always a good idea, since you never know what power tools or appliances you may need to use outdoors.

Water Requirements

Are you going to run a hose to your greenhouse, use a well or have a tap installed? Do you want a misting system with a timer, or are you content to hand water your plants with a watering can? If you plan to go on vacation, travel, or must be away for extended periods of time, you do not want to be a hostage to your greenhouse, so you may want to consider a timed watering system

On a hot day, you will be amazed just how rapidly your greenhouse can go from tropical humidity to being dry as a bone. Drip irrigation can help prevent this by adding a large water drum. The drum will also help retain heat during cool nights.

Greenhouses need water, and if you do not install a tap, your greenhouse should not be far from a water source. If you plan to use a watering can carried from the house, you should be prepared for many trips.

Price

I have seen few industries where there are such large discrepancies in prices for manufactured products. I have seen almost identically configured greenhouses vary as much in price as 200% or more. There are many large and small manufacturers, and the selection can be staggering. You have to weigh the factors that are important for you. For instance, some greenhouses have no base. Building your own base can often cost more than the greenhouse, after you factor in what your time is worth. I highly recommend writing and visiting as many greenhouse vendors as you can. Most gardening publications have a large selection of ads from greenhouse companies. If you are a handyman with construction skills, you are in luck. There are several books available on building your own greenhouse, and you may be able to save a lot of money and have greater latitude in the design and construction of your structure.

A greenhouse addition to an existing building need not be expensive or elaborate in order to be functional and practical.
(Martin P. Waterman photo.)

Once you know the requirements that are valuable to you, you can start to narrow down the list of possible greenhouses that have the features which you need. I have received many questions regarding greenhouses. My advice to most people who want one is to start with a small, inexpensive greenhouse, and see how you like it. This will initiate you into greenhouse growing, give you a better understanding of it, and guide you on how much you may wish to expand.

When you calculate price, do not forget the extra expenses. For instance, if you order a kit, how much will the freight and taxes cost? Be aware of the items the greenhouse you are buying does not have. Many greenhouse manufacturers offer an inexpensive stripped down model. However, once you begin to add in the extras, you may no longer have an inexpensive greenhouse.

Planning Hints

Planning is crucial, so I recommend the following: Make a list of what you would like to grow in the greenhouse. Tomatoes? Okay, how many plants? Are ten or fifteen enough? How many different varieties should be grown? How big will the pots be, or how much room will they take? Keep adding to your list, and you will get an idea of how much room you will need. If you are like most people, when you finish your list, you will probably need a greenhouse about the size of a football field. Now is the time for compromise, in order to bring the size down to suit your budget and reality. This exercise should tell you much about the type and size that best suits your needs. And, of course, you must remember that needs evolve.

You can find ads for greenhouses in gardening, home repair and other magazines. It is a wise idea to see who in your area is building greenhouses. Also, check the Yellow Pages for commercial greenhouses. There are some very economically priced models that can get you started. With some of the hoop greenhouses, you can add on 15-foot sections as you need them.

An important factor for the self-sufficiency gardener to consider is that it is possible to pay for your greenhouse in one season. If are able to sell several thousand bedding plants at a couple dollars a flat, well... you see what I mean.

Recommended Reading

Secrets to a Successful Greenhouse Business: A Complete Guide to Starting and Operating a

High Profit Business That's Beneficial to the Environment by T.M Taylor, Box 243, Melbourne, Florida 32902, 1991. ISBN 0-9628678-0-2. How to grow cash crops fast with your greenhouse, plus plans to build the greenhouse and market your plants.

The Hydroponic Hot House: Low-Cost, High-Yield Greenhouse Gardening by James B. DeKorne. Loompanics Unlimited, 1992. ISBN 1-55950-079-4. This book features much useful and pragmatic information and ideas which include alternative energy sources and numerous methods to increase your harvests.

The Homeowner's Complete Handbook for Add-On Solar Greenhouses & Sunspaces by Andrew M. Shapiro. Rodale Press, Inc., 1984. ISBN 0-87857-507-3. One of the best books on the subject, this book details what is necessary to add a greenhouse and sunspace onto your home, and spells out the advantages.

Chapter Nine

Hydroponic Gardening

The phrase "high-tech gardening" usually refers to the use of methods that utilize modern equipment such as computers or recently developed techniques to increase the yields and efficiency of food production. Unfortunately, high-tech gardening is often a misnomer, since many of the "new" technology systems, such as hydroponics, have been around for thousands of years.

Regardless of the label one wants to put on methods or systems that can be employed to make their food production systems more effective and efficient, a large percentage of growers naturally want to graduate to the next step in food production. This is particularly true when you are becoming more self-sufficient and earning money from your growing enterprise.

One of the most exciting aspects of hydroponic growing is that the prices for many systems are coming down. Also, once you have a basic under-standing of how these systems work, you can usually construct your own, often with simple and easily procured materials.

Understanding Hydroponics

Hydroponics, the science of growing plants without soil, is a viable alternative to cultivation using conventional methods. One particular suburban Chicago-area indoor hydroponic farm has operators who make a very impressive statement concerning the results they are achieving. They claim that they can produce the same amount of produce that would normally require 10 acres of greenhouse space or 100 acres of farmland. This indoor hydroponic farm can do this in an area consisting of only 10,000 square feet.

Despite the many advantages associated with hydroponic systems, very few people are taking advantage of this technology. One of the reasons for this is that most people do not understand hydroponics.

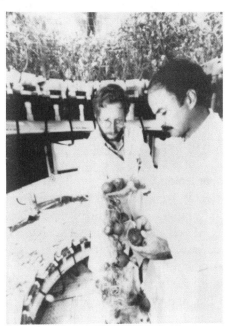

Hydroponics research is continually improving yields and methods. Here NASA scientists study systems that would feed astronauts on long journeys such as trips to Mars and beyond.
(NASA photo.)

Because we tend to fear the things we do not understand, many who could be benefiting from this technology do not do so simply because the misinformation and intimidation associated with these systems can be overwhelming. The fact that suppliers often glamorize the products and sometimes market them as super-high technology equal to the microchip or the space shuttle probably discourages more potential users than it encourages.

As simple as the process of hydroponics may be, the means of getting results can take several forms. There are many different types of systems, growing media, nutrient solutions and procedures, so trying to judge which system may be the best can often be overwhelming.

There is no point in using a hydroponic system just for the sake of being involved with hydroponics. What I am saying is that you should think carefully before you put a great deal of time, money and effort into a system. The following considerations should be reviewed, as they can help you to evaluate whether you can benefit from hydroponics, and if you can, the types of results you can expect from this new wave of gardening. As you read through these considerations, try to compare the advantages and disadvantages with the existing growing systems with which you are familiar.

Efficiency and Effectiveness

In order to know if a hydroponic system is for you, you will have to be able to judge if it will be more efficient and effective than your conventional mode of gardening.

Efficiency is the relationship that exists between inputs and outputs. There are two ways to increase efficiency. If you achieve a greater output for a given input, you have increased efficiency. If you can get the same output with less input, you have also increased efficiency. So, what does this mean to the grower? For one thing, it may mean the difference between merely scraping by, or earning a substantial amount of money with your system.

Efficiency is important, but so is effectiveness. When you are effective, this usually means that you are able to achieve your goals, which could be year-round food production. It could also mean that you are looking to increase profits by marketing more of your produce, especially during times when produce prices are high. The time you spend doing a little

research and talking to other hydroponic growers will be invaluable.

Hydroponic systems can vary so much in cost, complexity and performance that there is no cut-and-dried set of rules to follow in this high-tech frontier. This is the reason that hydroponics creates such a hard choice for so many people; they need to know what they want from a system that they usually do not understand.

What to Grow

Before you even start, spend some time planning the items you want to grow. If your Number One objective is self-sufficiency, then you want to grow those crops that are consistent with your plans for a reliable food production system. If you want to sell some of your produce, commercial considerations will have to be factored into your planning.

Of course, what you grow will have an influence on the type of system and medium you will be using, as well as where you will be using it. If you are growing in a greenhouse, you may also need a heating and/or cooling system. Also, if you are growing indoors, a lighting system will probably be necessary. When you know the crop you will be growing, you will know what it requires in order to achieve maximum productivity.

Once you know the crop you want to grow, try to find people who are growing these crops hydroponically to learn who is having the best success, and take note of the type of systems they are using.

Learn from Others

Since there are so many different systems available, including those that can be constructed, the best advice I can give is to tell you to go talk to others. If there are some commercial operations in your area, visit them. Ask many questions, such as "What would you do differently if you had to do it all over again?" Try to find out which are the most popular systems in your area, and why that is so. You do not want to end up with one particular system, and then find that you really need a different type.

It is very important to talk to as many sources as you can. Hydroponics is like a religion to many growers. There are many philosophies, factions and interpretations, and you may get several different opinions on any particular topic. However, you have to choose a system that is right for you, and in doing your leg work and research, you should find yourself gravitating to a system that suits your objectives and lifestyle.

Active or Passive

Hydroponic systems are classified by how the nutrients are to be delivered to the root system. Passive systems use a wick and, therefore, complexity is rather low, since there are no moving parts. The cost is reasonable, especially for someone just trying to get their feet wet, so to speak.

Active systems usually use a reservoir of some type. There are many types of active systems. Some of them re-use nutrient solutions (recovery system), and some of them do not (non-recovery systems).

Active Systems

There are three major types of active systems. The flood-and-drain systems do just as they say. They flood the bed with a nutrient rich solution, which then drains away. The flooding action helps to remove the CO^2-rich air from the bed, and when the nutrient levels recede, it draws fresh oxygenated air back into the growing medium. There are many flood and drain systems which can be purchased in several many different sizes and configurations. Flood-and-drain systems are now called "ebb-and-flow" systems by most manufacturers.

The top-feed method relies on the application of the nutrient solution directly to the base of each plant via small feeder tubes and a pump.

The nutrient film technique (NFT) is a very productive type of system that is capable of producing large yields. The reason for this is that nutrients are constantly being cycled over the roots that grow in a light-tight tube. There is no medium with this system, which is an advantage. However, if you experience a power interruption, you can lose or have extreme damage to your crop, which is a distinct disadvantage. NFT was developed in England for areas with poor soil quality and an inadequate water supply.

Because there is no medium to support the roots, a support system is necessary for plants such as tomatoes and cucumbers.

Another problem associated with an NFT system is that it does not always provide adequate oxygen to the plant's roots, since there is continuous nutrient flow. The problem is caused when large root masses slow and actually stop the flow of water, which in turn causes the plants to quickly use up the supply of oxygen. Currently, there are systems under development and testing which would vary the cycle times and use other technology to overcome this problem. One test, in which a timer was used to turn on and off the NFT system at 30-minutes intervals, resulted in a much faster growth rate for the plants.

Perhaps aero-hydroponics represents the direction in which the science is heading. With this system, the roots are misted with an oxygen-enriched solution. Developed in Israel, aero-hydroponics has been effective for use in plant propagation, particularly with hard to propagate woody plants. One of the benefits of this system is that there is no growing medium.

Aero-hydroponic systems are expensive, because they involve more pumps and sprayers than other systems. However, operating costs are low, and with the high yield, these could be systems to consider, if you have the investment money with which to start.

No Soil — No Toil?
The Growing Medium

A growing medium is used to support a root system and to hold the nutrients, water and oxygen needed for plant growth. While some systems use a growing medium, others do not. Some forms of growing medium will need to be replaced, and some types can interact with the nutrients so that some extra care and monitoring is necessary. There are many types of media available including gravel, sand-crushed brick, sawdust and rockwool.

If you live near a sawmill, you may be able to use sawdust. Because wood is often treated before it is milled, the sawdust can harbor contaminants which can have a detrimental effect on your plants.

Rockwool, a fibrous form of rock, is becoming extremely popular and should be considered.

Rockwool was developed in Denmark and Holland, and represents a leap forward from the early gravel systems. Rockwool is produced when basaltic rock is heated and spun (something like cotton candy) to produce a porous and sterile medium for plants, although one of rockwool's more popular uses has been for insulation.

As popular as rockwool is, it does have its drawbacks. The fibers are a health hazard, and caution should be employed (face mask, goggles and gloves) when handling it before it becomes wet. Rockwool is nonbiodegradable, and salts can also build up to toxic levels.

Nutrient Solutions

You can make nutrient solutions yourself, or you can purchase nutrient solutions. If you purchase your nutrient solutions, you are becoming dependent on a supplier who may not always be there. Making your own solutions is the best way, but there is nothing wrong with starting and learning with a commercial solution until you get the feel of using a hydroponic system. By using a commercial solution, you will be ensured of a balanced nutrient formula.

If you do make your own formulas, you have to be careful not to introduce large particles which can potentially clog up your system. An excellent book is *Hydroponic Nutrients: Easy Ways to Make Your Own* by M. Edward Muckle. It is available from Grower's Press, which also publishes the *21st Century Gardener* magazine. Because the science of hydroponics is dependent upon the nutrient solutions, an understanding of solution components and their effects is necessary if you are to reap maximum benefits from any system.

The type of nutrient formula and the concentrations will depend on what you grow. Lettuce are light feeders, as are most herbs; and require about 700-900 ppm. (parts per million) of nutrients. Tomatoes, peppers and spinach are heavy feeders, and these will need a heavier concentration of nutrients, or about 900-1,100 ppm.

Excessive heat can cause evaporation which can quickly bring ppm's to a toxic level. Depending on your system and environment, you will need to take this into consideration.

CO^2 Systems

Many hydroponic supply houses offer CO^2 systems to fertilize the air, and they make claims of doubled growth and flowering. The resulting growth can be so dramatic that the plants have to be cut back. If you want such a system, you will have to rent a tank and probably have it filled every three months or so.

There are also CO^2 generators. These systems use a propane tank and burn the gas to create CO^2. The generators come in various sizes, depending on how many cubic feet per hour of CO^2 you need to produce.

Time and Resources

There are numerous questions to be asked in this regard. Are you going to do all the maintenance, planting and harvesting yourself, or is someone else? How much time can you devote to your system? Could you go away for several weeks or a month without too much trouble? How much power is it going to consume vs. what it is going to produce? What is the expected life of your system? How much maintenance will it require? How often will the growing media be replaced? How dependable are your sources of nutrient solution?

Organic Considerations

There are some people who believe that social responsibility is very important, and they are willing to absorb some financial cost in order to protect the environment. Hydroponic growing fosters organic growing in two ways. First, conventional farming, especially with heavy applications of chemical fertilizers, results in a loss of beneficial bacteria and earthworms. This chemical run off is also an environmental hazard. Pest control in conventional farming, even in a small area, can require tons of pesticides, herbicides and fungicides, which are often applied each and every year.

Organic hydroponics represents an increasing segment of the industry. Organic nutrients such as worm castings, fish waste, seaweed extracts and various manures are being employed, and this is expected to continue.

There has been some controversy over the dumping of spent nutrient solutions. This concern has contributed to the lessened popularity of non-recycling systems for hydroponics.

Indoors or Out

Hydroponic systems are suited for use indoors, in greenhouses and for use outdoors. Most applications are being done indoors. Hydroponic systems, when properly designed and instituted, take up less space than conventional gardening methods. By growing in an indoor environment, pests can be eliminated. This means that in some instances you can grow your produce organically.

If your system is to be installed in a greenhouse, you will have to know something about greenhouses and may have to consider such things as fans and blowers, coverings and other related items.

If your hydroponic system is indoors or in a greenhouse, you may have to hand-pollinate some of your crops in order to produce fruit and vegetables.

If your system is in your home, you may have to deal with a problem that no one really mentions which can arise from a hydroponic system... and that is the smell. If you have an indoor system, you may want to go easy on home brew nutrients such as manure tea, and stick to solutions that will be more nose-friendly. You may also need a ventilation system as well as a fan to keep air circulating.

Test Equipment

There is no shortage of test equipment available for the hydroponic grower. There are pH meters, moisture meters, light meters, CO_2 test kits and parts-per-million meters, just to name a few. pH testing is important to monitor acidity and alkalinity. pH testing is also important if you use rockwool, since it tends to raise the pH of the nutrient solution.

One of the best pieces of test equipment is your eye. If you develop a good eye, you can spot deficiencies that your plants will often exhibit. Plants are usually not shy in telling you when something is out of sync. The trick is to diagnose it early on, when they are giving the subtle hints and the problems are still reversible.

Buy vs. Build

The are many small systems which can be purchased that will have you up and running quickly. Whether you buy or build will have a dramatic effect on the cost of your system. It is true that a futuristic looking system with tubes, lights, bells and whistles is impressive and can make you look like the neighborhood high-tech wizard. If you install such a system, it can be a model of institutional efficiency. However, hydroponic systems can be built that will equal or surpass many of the top-of-the-line systems.

Whether you buy or build, an invaluable book is *Basic Hydroponics: Hydroponics for the Do-it-Yourselfer*. The science of hydroponics, from inception to modern-day techniques, is described in a manner that will enable readers to understand the science and build their own systems. This book is available from the *21st Century Gardener*.

Cleanliness

This is a double-edged sword. Hydroponic systems do not have to use soil, so you do not have to look as if you are auditioning for a Tide commercial after your gardening chores. A level of cleanliness is necessary in hydroponics, however, since using water to deliver nutrients means that a certain level of sanitation is necessary to prevent algae from forming.

Lighting Systems

There are many types of lighting which can be used, and time spent on research will be time well-spent. For example, four different kinds of high-intensity discharge (HID) lights are available. These are mercury vapor (seldom used but inexpensive), metal halide (UV radiation can be harmful, so care is needed), high-pressure sodium (excellent, and especially good for rooms with low ceilings) and low-pressure sodium (efficient commercial light, but costly). With any lighting system, you will need a timer.

Some form of lighting system is clearly required, and this can cost some money in the form of the fixtures, bulbs and increase in your electricity bill. These outlays all have to be balanced with your projected increase in yield or personal enjoyment.

Another aspect of artificial lighting is that it now has been proven that some people suffer from seasonal affective disorders (SAD) during winter, and that light exposure decreases depression, fatigue, loss of interest in sex, anxiety, weight gain and other SAD-related problems. So, another advantage of a hydroponic system with artificial lighting would be brightening up your winter emotionally.

Start Small

There are many advantages to hydroponic systems. One of the key advantages is that some hydroponic systems will allow you to start small and then add. You may want to try one of the "closet systems," and after you experience the requirements and have had a taste of your harvest, you can judge if you want to expand, or maybe even employ a different type of system. One result of my research is the discovery that anyone who has started with a hydroponic system has become very attached to it. I hesitate to use the word "addicted," but I have found that a close relationship or bond can often form between a person and their system.

By starting small you can get the bugs out. You can get a feeling for the scheduling of planting, maintenance and harvesting, and if you plan on selling produce, you can have a chance to build a customer base that can help you to finance your expansion.

Commercial Considerations

In my area there are many hydroponic operations springing up. Our produce prices are high, since it is primarily imported from the southern United States, Mexico and other warmer climates. Many of these operations have the latest equipment that the hydroponic sciences can offer. Also, many receive government grants, and I think this is in part due to the fact that government bureaucrats are impressed with the potential of this new technology.

Commercial food growing for the hydroponic grower usually means meeting the seasonal demand when prices are high. This means growing during the colder months when conventional outdoor operations cannot function. Hydroponic systems are also viable in areas where there is a shortage of water, or very poor soils.

If the commercial aspect of hydroponic culture interests you, talk to some produce managers and see what they would like and when they would like it. I have found that produce managers love buying fresh local produce. They are ecstatic when they can get a constant supply of an item that their customers are demanding. Most supermarkets depend on their produce sections to make much of their profit, and are always looking for advantages in price and quality, as well as unique products. Hydroponic growers can usually produce a superior looking product, as well as an organic product. When you go to talk with produce managers and restaurant food purchasers, bring plenty of samples for them to taste.

Foolproof Systems?

Many systems are advertised as foolproof, low maintenance, user-friendly and so on. Don't take anyone's word about how good a system may be, particularly that of a salesperson whose primary interest is in selling a system. Arm yourself with knowledge. If you ask enough questions and then try to verify the facts with enough people, you will soon be able to know the type of system that will suit your goals, lifestyle and budget. A salesperson is concerned with the sale. You have to be concerned with your own interests.

This brings up another point: Only deal with a reputable dealer who offers some type of warranty. Some dealers in systems and supplies work part-time, and some sell from their homes to help support their hobbies. There is nothing wrong with this, providing they are there to help you if your system develops problems.

The Future Of Hydroponics

Hydroponics is a young science and is rapidly changing. The systems available are developing and becoming more efficient. There are now vertical NFT systems that can save space and produce high yields by growing lettuce or other plants on something that looks like a tree. Solutions continue to evolve, as do new lighting systems.

Because commercial growers and universities are becoming more involved with hydroponics, there are bound to be continual breakthroughs. Hydroponics is growing throughout the world, and there will be additional new developments, especially as technology that is in use in European and other foreign countries becomes more refined.

Hydroponic systems are being used on the Russian space station, as well as at the United States Antarctic Research Station at the South Pole. In desert climates, where water is scarce, hydroponic systems allow high-yield crops to be produced using very little water, since it is recycled. As hydroponic systems become more popular, they will come down in price. As more commercial operations spring up, so will systems for the small grower.

Recommended Reading

Basic Hydroponics for the Do-It-Yourselfer: A Cultural Handbook by M. Edward Muckle. Growers Press Inc., 1994, ISBN 0-921981-40-6. Highly recommended reading for anyone practicing hydroponics, by one of the top experts on the planet.

Hydroponic Nutrients: Easy Ways to Make Your Own by M. Edward Muckle. Growers Press Inc., 1993. ISBN 0-921981-33-3. Create your own nutrient formulas to save money and become more self-sufficient.

Chapter Ten

Computer Gardening and the Internet

Computer Gardening

Computer programs for the gardener are available in two important forms. The first is software which makes the whole exercise of growing food more efficient, effective and, yes, even more fun. The second type of computer gardening is communicating with other gardeners and farmers through an on-line service or on the Internet.

There are many software packages which are ideal for the gardener and farmer. They are available on computer disk or CD-ROM, which means that you may have to invest in a computer and maybe even a back-up power supply.

The value of gardening software should not be underestimated. As a general rule, look for three components in any gardening related software program that you purchase. The first component is an educational feature such as a plant encyclopedia or database that will help you learn more about gardening. The second component is a feature that will help you draw plans for your garden so you can conceptualize and execute the project correctly. The third component to look for is a scheduling feature which allows you to plan maintenance such as pruning, watering and fertilizing based on the types of plant material that you have selected.

If you are looking at the market and are thinking about purchasing a used computer, you will probably quickly learn that some computer systems don't have the power to run in the Microsoft Windows environment. These older systems can often be purchased for less than two hundred dollars, often with a monitor and a printer. There are many gardening and communication applications that will run on this type of hardware, and this could be an excellent and inexpensive way to get into computer gardening.

Choosing the Best Gardening Software

Landscape software comes in many different shapes and forms. There is a logical explanation for this. Much of the available software represents a convergence of two types of computer programs. At the high end of the market, computer-aided design programs are becoming easier to use and available in specialized pared-down versions for specific tasks such as landscaping. At the bottom end of the market, many simple programs that have been used for light projects such as gardening and simple drawing and designing have blossomed into powerful applications. A third section of the market is CD-ROM's. They have blended design features and catalogs of plant material to give gardeners and landscapers a wide palette of information and plant material to consider when planning their gardens.

In order to choose the best gardening software for your needs, you will first have to examine what they are. Of course, gardening software may well quickly change your conception of your needs and redefine the objectives you are trying to accomplish.

It is probably best to start with a product that is in your price range and promises to expose you to many ideas and philosophies, while at the same time giving you a suitable tool for designing and understanding your gardening environment. Of course, you will also have to consider the type of hardware you have available.

One of the things that amazes me about gardening software is the speed with which you can start and complete a design using landscape software. I was able to draw my heavily landscaped property, complete with every tree, bush, flower bed and all the other items (picnic table, car, pickup truck, chairs, barbecue, etc.) in less than 20 minutes. After that, I was running "what if?" scenarios by trying different plantscape and hardscape materials and dropping them into my plan.

I also made some additions to my orchard on the computer which I will be executing over the next few years. Another important feature I discovered is that by having a map of all the fruit trees, fruit bushes and other plant material that you are growing, you will find it easier to keep a record of the varieties in your garden. For instance, if you have 20-30 or more different apple varieties, you probably will never be able to remember what they are, since plant labels and tags only last a few seasons.

Many of the programs are focused on landscaping and while the tools are probably most often used for flower beds and ornamental work, the same tools are ideal for garden and farm plot design. Practically all landscape software is customizable, so you can add your own plants and other items to the databases.

Landscape software has allowed many entrepreneurial growers to get into the landscape business. The software gives you a powerful tool with which to show prospective customers how their property will look when the landscaping is completed. Changes are as simple as deleting material and pointing and clicking to add new material. This can be done in seconds, as the drawing does not have to be started from scratch.

Owing to the renewed interest in America's favorite pastime and the increasing popularity of computers, many companies are making gardening software. A few companies and their products are listed and described in the pages that follow.

Abracadata

Design Your Own Home: Landscape is aimed at the large home owner market and is definitely an entry level program. Although there are better choices for the professional landscaper, there are some that do use this program. *Design your Own Home: Landscape* gives you the ability to display your landscape plan from five different perspectives: right,

left, front, back and overhead. It also allows you to age your landscape. The graphics for this program tend to be very simplistic and often cartoon-like. One of the drawbacks of all landscaping and gardening software is that programs do not render plant material well enough for it to be easily be identified.

Design Your Own Home: Landscape does offer a wide variety of ground surfaces and textures, so that you can add your mulch, patio bricks, coarse stone or whatever your favorite medium may be. After you have designed your landscape, you can print a plant list with this program.

Abracadata does offer the widest selections of formats for its landscaping program, and it is available for DOS, Windows, Mac, Apple II and Apple IIGS systems. Abracadata specializes in plan-making software and that includes their *Interiors and Architecture* design programs.

Abracadata also makes a gardening program that is simple and fun to use. It is very practical and an excellent educational tool for those who want to learn more about gardening.

Sprout! is available in DOS, Windows or Macintosh versions and does not take very much power to run. There are many innovative features incorporated into this program, the best being the fact that you can quickly and easily design a garden. Tell the program the hardiness zone in which you are located and it will automatically suggest to you when to plant and the types of plants that you can grow. The program also automatically and accurately spaces your seeds to the recommended allowances so you will know how much seed to order. This makes the program a perfect companion to your seed catalogs when you are contemplating the items you should plant for the next growing season.

Sprout! can also generate a number of reports such as the size of the harvest that you can expect. While the program cannot anticipate weather or crop failure, this is a useful feature, and in time you can compensate in those areas where the computer is slightly off the mark due to details it does not have. I found this feature to be fairly accurate as a general rule, however.

Also included with the program is comprehensive growing information, so that you can learn more about gardening and the items you are planting. From the plant database, click on beets (for instance) and you will be shown the planting time, time to germinate, time to harvest, soil pH required, spacing between plants and rows, depth to plant seeds and the height of the mature plant. There is also other information available. For instance, under the beet heading it will tell you interesting information about beets — for example: young greens can be harvested and eaten. I was surprised at how accurate the planting times were for my area and how it matched the information in seed catalogs and that of my personal experience.

This planning tool is ideal because you can run "what if?" scenarios. You will probably get several gardening ideas from the computer since you can explore options and new varieties from the very comprehensive plant lists. If you choose something that you have never grown previously, the information you need is readily available at your fingertips.

There are powerful drawing tools available so that you can customize your garden any way you like. You can also add new vegetables and other plants to the database and then edit to reflect the way in which you garden.

You can print your garden plans on one page or tile them so that they fit up to 8 pages. Since the computer calculates yields, you can decide how much produce you want and then use the planning tools to design your garden to obtain this result.

At the time of writing, if you order directly from Abracadata, the price is $59.95 for this program. As with the price of any software, it pays first to compare the price charged by your local retailers, then call some of the many discount software vendors that advertise in computer magazines.

AutoSketch

Home Series Landscape is a relatively easy-to-use gardening program, as it was designed for the homeowner. There are also many landscape professionals who have chosen to use this particular program.

Home Series Landscape is not a complicated program and the literature states you should be up and running within thirty minutes. However, this program may be one of the tougher ones to master. It is not difficult to learn, it just takes time to learn the features. If you have experience using DOS-based CAD programs, *Home Series Landscape* is a snap.

The 3-D viewer gives this DOS program an exciting element whereby you can look at your renderings from different angles. The program also generates a shopping list which can be exported to a spreadsheet, estimator program or other programs.

I had expected the manual to be difficult, this being a CAD program. I was surprised to find it very straight forward and easy to understand.

Consistent with its larger CAD cousins, this is a precision-design program in every sense, you can create great designs that are accurate within 1/16th of an inch. *Home Series Landscape* is also designed to work together with the other *Home Series* programs. This is an advantage, because once you are proficient with *Landscape*, you can use other AutoSketch Home Series programs such as *Home, Kitchen & Bath* and *Deck*.

Books That Work

One of the hot new titles for gardeners is a program called *3-D Landscape*. It is from a company called Books That Work which has some other useful titles that show you how to do your own plumbing and electrical work. *3-D Landscape* has received a good share of exposure in the computer press and other media because of its ease of use and exciting 3-dimensional renderings.

This power comes with a price. You can run the program on an IBM 386 machine, but you will probably find that the program runs very slowly. A 486 or a Pentium powered computer is really the level for which this program was designed.

3-D Landscape comes with a library of 400 different plants. One interesting feature is "Shadow Caste," which allows you to decide where the shade will fall as the sun crosses the sky. You'll be able to know if you will need to plant shade-tolerant or sun-loving plants by seeing how much sun and shade they are likely to receive. There is also a multimedia how-to guide to provide you with the fundamentals of landscaping and layout.

I got the feeling that 3-D Landscape was a good product but needed to be refined by enlarging its plant libraries and sample gardens. But, the price can't be beat, especially if you are not seeking a high-end professional product.

Green Thumb Software

LandDesigner and *LandDesigner Pro* are the two programs available from Green Thumb Software. There are both DOS and Windows versions, but there is no version for the Mac and none is planned.

All the Green Thumb products are easy-to-use, yet come packed with powerful features. *LandDesigner* for DOS could be an excellent starting point for those who want to explore these types of programs. Now that the price has been reduced to $39, it does not represent much financial risk, yet it has powerful features, such as being able to generate a materials list and cost projection for each project. You can also design an irrigation or sprinkler system and then turn it on to see if it will provide adequate coverage.

This program can be used for designing a landscape for a property as large as 170 acres. If you like this program, *LandDesigner Pro* for DOS is the logical upgrade, featuring higher-quality presentation drawings, faster editing, larger irrigation layouts and expanded plant selections. The comprehensive plant libraries also allow you to generate a comprehensive plant list which has 20 fields of information for each plant. *LandDesigner* and *LandDesigner Pro* for DOS will also support over 300 different printers.

LandDesigner and *LandDesigner Pro* for Windows are for those who prefer working in the Windows environment. Of course, you will need much more computer power to run the program, but you are also gaining some extra capabilities. The on-line help in Windows is easy to use, and the program has a very similar feel and look to its DOS predecessor, as well as the same tools, such as being able to generate materials lists and cost projections.

One of the best things about the Windows versions is the on-line tutorial which is very thorough and includes everything from getting help, to how to design and test the sprinkler systems. If you are new to the Windows environment, there is even a tutorial on how to use Windows features, so that you can be up and running quickly. I wish that all the design programs had built-in tutorials such as these.

LandDesigner Pro for Windows is the top-of-the-line software from Green Thumb. It has the ability to generate elevation views. In *LandDesigner Pro* you get 300 symbols, but you can also create your own symbols and add them to the symbol library. *LandDesigner Pro* has been well received by the

landscape trade, and most of the users of the DOS version have indicated that they will be switching to the Windows version.

Extra libraries are sold separately, and there is a discount if you purchase two or more libraries.

Green Thumb Software has also released its *LandDesigner Multi-Media for Gardens*. At the core of this CD-ROM is Green Thumb's high-quality landscaping program. To bring the landscaping features to gardeners, Green Thumb Software paired up with White Flower Farm, which contributed over 1,000 full color photo images.

This program is feature rich, and although I would like to have seen much more plant material in the database, this program is powerful, fun to employ and anticipates the direction in which garden design software is heading.

Land Designer Multi-Media for Gardens uses the familiar Windows interface, which is easy to use. The databases are very thorough, which makes planning a pleasure. One feature that I truly appreciate is that you can listen to the narrative and learn how to pronounce the plant names. If you are stumped for ideas, there are templates that you can use and amend to your particular tastes. There is also a comprehensive set of drawing tools, and with them you can create a garden up to 170 acres in size. This product is basically *LandDesigner* for Windows with all kinds of goodies so that it will appeal to gardeners. In this, the company has succeeded in producing a first-class product that along with being practical, is fun and educational.

Lifestyle Software Group

Garden Companion CD is built around a gardening system designed to help you choose the best plants for your site as well as providing you with a maintenance schedule for the plants you choose. The CD comes with an encyclopedia of 1,000 plants with 43 cultivation requirements. I know that this is already sounding like too much work, but at least this program does not hide the fact that plants and gardens do need maintenance.

The photographs are of high quality and are provided by Derek Fell, one of the most famous garden photographers in North America.

The program is heavily weighted on the landscape end. However, there is so much gardening information in its database that this is a CD-ROM worth investigating. If you want to do some serious landscaping, there is a feature that enables you to choose from ten garden designs. These include Victorian, Elizabethan, formal, historic, Japanese and English country gardens.

Gardening and software programs are continually being upgraded and released, and these are tools that can save money and introduce the user to new ideas. Software prices are continually falling, and this will make programs such as those mentioned available at even lower prices.

Gardening and Farming on the Internet

If you have not heard of the Internet, or information superhighway, you probably are already living in the woods. There are many resources on the Internet that the self-sufficiency gardener will find useful and possibly even mandatory.

One of the advantages of an external modem is that they are easy to configure. This particular model will let you send and receive faxes and comes with software that will turn your computer into an answering machine.
(Boca Research, Inc. photo.)

There are many things that you need to consider before you can connect. The first is a computer and a modem. The second is a provider whose fees will not bankrupt you. Fortunately, the cost of becoming a provider is coming down and therefore there is heavy competition for users as firms enter the Internet provider business.

Sometimes you can get onto the Internet for free. Certain areas are blessed with FreeNets. These are created under the same philosophy as your local library; namely, that information should be free to all who want it. Unfortunately, at this time there are not many FreeNets, and, some have limited services. Fortunately, most have the two most important services that you need: e-mail and USENET News.

Internet in Brief

Each month about one million people hop on the Infobahn or, as it is more commonly known, the information superhighway. Probably about half of them are searching for entertainment, while the other half are business users. The amount of information on the Internet is staggering. One of the keys to success is knowing what you are looking for and where to find it. There is so much information available that is useful for the gardener. I have found many sources of free information and even plant material. The Internet is relatively uncensored, and you can also talk to people over your computer, using the keyboard and employing what is known as IRC or international relay chat. This gives you an opportunity to find out what is going on in different countries and cultures without interpretation from the news or print media. For instance, Internet users knew almost instantly when war had broken out in the Persian Gulf. The Internet is proving to be a very efficient way of keeping on top of issues that may affect you and your loved ones. Below are some of the features that will appeal to the self-sufficiency gardener, and ones that you may want to consider using.

News Groups

Simply put, news groups are Internet discussion groups between people from around the planet. The topics cover practically any subject that you can imagine.

There are over 10,000 news groups, but since many are in foreign languages, most providers will give you about 5,000 or so.

You can tell much about the type of news group by its prefix.

"alt": alternative subjects, practically anything goes.
"biz": business-related news groups.
"comp": computer-related topics.
"sci": usually relates to scientific topics.

"soc": social issues and socializing.

"talk": usually debate and discussion oriented forums.

"news": associated with USENET and news group issues.

"rec": for recreational and hobby activities.

I often have questions about gardening and related topics. One day I cut open a squash to bake, and wondered if the seeds were edible and could be prepared in the same manner as pumpkin seeds, a close relative. I posted the question in the rec.gardens news group, and within minutes I had answers from around the world. I was still receiving replies weeks later. Not only did I find they were edible, but I received different recipes from Europe and all over North America.

You do not have to post questions to use the newsgroups; you can simply read the questions and responses of others. This is called "lurking."

I have met many people through news groups with whom I communicate regularly. We exchange ideas, information and even plant material. It gives me a feeling of security, knowing that when I need information on pests, diseases, material or anything you can imagine, I can have an assortment of answers and opinions in no time.

When using the Internet and newsgroups, there is a certain etiquette which is called "netiquette." For instance, it is frowned upon to use the news groups or e-mail to solicit business. You are likely to get "flamed," which is receiving angry letters in your electronic mail box.

Before you use a news group, it is a good idea to lurk for a while and get a feel for it. Most news groups will have a FAQ or frequently asked questions document. This eliminates repetitive questions from new people to the Internet, or those who are new to the particular group. These new users are often referred to as "newbies."

For instance, in the FAQ for misc.survivalism, the group is described as follows: "more than just a list of questions and answers, FAQ's are short introductions to the community that subscribe to the newsgroup. In misc.survivalism, we discuss survival theory. If there was one line we could lift out of our charter to sum up the group, it would be, the prevailing philosophy of misc.survivalism is that I and the ones I love want to remain alive no matter what."

The rest of the FAQ deals with emergency preparedness as well as do's and don'ts. For instance,

if you don't like guns you are better off in a news group such as talk.politics.guns. If all you want to talk about is guns, you should go to rec.guns. FAQ's may also contain some history about a news group. For example, misc.survivalism had over 400 people vote for the creation of this group, which brings up another important topic. If you have a new idea for a group that is different from any that exist, there is a mechanism to start one.

There are probably over 100 news groups that are of interest to the self-sufficiency gardener. I will comment on a few of the most obvious and helpful ones shown below.

The first is *rec.gardens,* the largest news group for gardeners and growers. If you have any question on plant material, pests or sources of supply, post a message on this group and you will probably get answers from around the world. I find that I use this for most of my gardening and related questions.

If you have any questions about preserving foods, there is a very useful news group called rec.preserving. It is particularly helpful during harvest time. The correct answer to a problem can often help pay for some of your Internet time.

If you like to cook or create value-added products, there are several news groups dealing with recipes and cooking tips. A few groups worth checking out are: rec.food.recipes, rec.food.veg, and rec.food.veg.cooking.

Two other groups are: alt.landscape.architecture, which deals with landscaping problems and solutions, while rec.ponds deals with backyard ponds.

Another gardening-related news group that I find useful quite often is alt.folklore.herbs. This news group deals with medicinal plant information, as well as herbal recipes and products.

If you are into heavy-duty gardening, there is sci.agriculture, alt.agriculture.fruit and misc.rural.

There are many other groups on gardening and related topics, as well as groups on alternative lifestyle and alternative energy sources. The USENET news groups are an inexpensive way to network with people all over the world who think the same way as you do.

World Wide Web

The World Wide Web is one of the fastest-growing and most popular areas of the Internet. The

World Wide Web links files and documents that pertain to a similar subject across different sites.

The WWW is turning into the commercial component of the net, and this is where people look to shop for any type of product, service or information available. There are still some problems with the WWW, such as security issues; thus, you should not give your credit card or personal information to anyone over the Internet.

There are many gardening sites on the WWW, and you can even browse back issues of some gardening magazines. There are many newspapers as well. One of the most popular destinations is finding weather information, usually in the form of a satellite map.

You can also search for information on farming, gardening and other topics on the WWW. There are other search tools such as Gopher and Archie that allow you to search for information at universities and government sites. This can result in obtaining much free information on horticulture and agriculture. Archie and Gopher software is usually part of any Internet software package.

E-Mail

E-mail is practically instantaneous, and once you start using it you will wonder why you used conventional (often dubbed "snail mail") postal services. Over thirty million people now have e-mail, and the number is continually growing. If you need information, a catalog or a reply to a letter, you can often have it in minutes. The manuscript for this book was e-mailed to the publisher, and much of the research was done on the WWW and USENET news groups. I am finding that I am using the Internet for enhancing many other facets of my life. I just hope that nobody blasts them durn satellites out of the sky.

Portable Internet and Falling Prices

One of the benefits of the computer age is that computers and software are increasingly becoming more affordable. On-line services are also dropping in price. I now use a laptop computer with rechargeable batteries. I can check my e-mail or hop on the Internet anywhere in North America or the world, as long as I have a telephone line to plug into. Information

technology is quickly changing. As I mentioned in the first chapter of this book, one of the keys to success is finding the information that you need to speed and simplify the process of self-sufficiency gardening. Computers and communication with others such as yourself is probably the best way to do it.

Software Sources

Abracadata
P. O. Box 2440
Eugene, OR 97402
1-800-451-4871
Design Your Own Home: Landscape, SPROUT!

Autodesk
18911 North Creek Parkway, Suite 105
Bothell, WA 98011
Toll free 1-800-228-3601
The Home Series Landscape

Books that Work
2300 Geng Road, Building 3, Suite 100
Palo Alto, CA 94303
1-800-242-4546
3-D Landscape

Green Thumb Software
75 Manhattan Drive, Suite 100
Boulder, CO 80303
1-800-336-3127
LandDesigner, LandDesigner Pro, Irrigator Pro, LandDesigner Multimedia for Windows

Lifestyle Software Group
63 Orange Street
St. Augustine, FL 32084
1-800-289-1157
Garden Companion CD

NetManage
10725 North De Anza Blvd.
Cupertino, CA 95014
1-408-973-7171
Makers of *Internet Chameleon* Software

Chapter Eleven

Seed Saving and Propagation

Seed propagation or saving seeds is one of the easiest ways to guarantee continuity of your gardening endeavors. It was a common practice among the early settlers to grow three separate gardens. The first garden was for fresh fruit and vegetables throughout the growing season. The second garden was for fruits and vegetables that were grown to be preserved and stored to sustain the families through the winter. The third and probably the most important garden was the seed garden, in which plants were allowed to go to seed so that there could be seeds for the following year's crop.

One of the basic and proven principles in making money is to buy low and sell high. In becoming self-sufficient through the crops you grow, the same principle applies. The lower you can keep your costs, the more profits you are likely to reap.

Zucchini is a fast growing and productive crop.
(Martin P. Waterman photo.)

Therefore, if you have a mechanism to create your own plant material, you can save hundreds, even thousands of dollars on seeds and other plants. For instance, if you know how to start certain plants from cuttings, you can multiply your food bearing stock very efficiently. Grape cuttings will root in moist soil with an almost 100% success rate. Contrast this with buying grape plants at $3-$10 each. If you want to add 100 grape vines, it could potentially cost you from $300 to $1,000 dollars. Obviously, propagating your own material can save you a lot of money. Many nurserymen got their start by growing their own material and then selling the excess plants to other growers, landscapers and hobbyists. It should come as no surprise that some gardeners make more money selling bedding plants than they do selling their harvests.

Starting your own seeds and plants has many benefits besides the obvious money savings. When you start your own plants, you have control over the quality and trueness of the material you grow. Too many times plants purchased from commercial establishments are mislabeled. Many nurseries are lax when it comes to labeling material, especially when it comes to fruit trees. You may ask for a Macintosh apple, but if they sell you a Northern Spy, you will not know until it fruits, which could be several years from the day you purchased the tree. If you purchase from a nursery or garden center, you could also be purchasing infected or just plain stunted material that has resulted from being grown in a manner in which it was not properly nourished, watered or tended. For instance, nursery material that has dried out may have lost much of its critical root mass. This could result in a plant that will be very slow-growing and prone to death or disease.

It is not uncommon to have plants that you start from cuttings or even seeds outperform one- or even two-year-old plants from some nurseries or garden centers. This material is often damaged and allowed to dry out. As is often the case with department store and other seasonal garden centers, the person who sells you those apple trees may be back to selling goldfish or appliances when the season is over.

Hybrid vs. Non-hybrid Seeds

As you peruse seed catalogs, you will see that many varieties are labeled as being hybrids. A hybrid plant is produced by the cross-pollination of two genetically different plants. Hybrids rarely come true from their seeds. For instance, if you purchase a hybrid tomato plant and then plant the seeds, the resulting offspring will probably not resemble the parent plant. Therefore, seeds from hybrid plants are rarely saved. Seeds of non-hybrid plants may also have to be isolated (bagged so that they self-pollinate) so that the plant's attributes can be given to successive generations. There are many texts on the subject of seed saving. Because there are so many different vegetable and other plant varieties, it is wise to invest in a book, since different plants have different requirements when it comes to saving their seeds. There are also many seed saving organizations, and their objective is usually to save non-hybrid plant seeds that are threatened by extinction because they are not being widely grown anymore.

Historic and Heirloom Seeds

The selection of seeds is phenomenal, with some, such as tomatoes and peppers, being available in hundreds of varieties. I like to think of seeds in two ways. There are the newer seeds that are offered each year, and then there are the older seeds, proven varieties, some of which have been used for generations. I prefer a combination of both.

Unfortunately for most gardeners, a seed is just a seed. Most people start by ordering them from the seed company or purchasing them from a local co-op or garden center. Then they put the seeds in the ground and up come the vegetables. However, the type of seed you grow can have a great effect on the flavor, yields, uses, and uniqueness of the produce you harvest and preserve.

These young cabbage will be harvested in the autumn and will keep until spring.
(Martin P. Waterman photo.)

Although historic and heirloom seeds can offer you a wider spectrum of varieties than can usually be grown, each variety you consider should be given a careful evaluation to see if it merits replacing an existing garden favorite. For every vegetable you can grow, there will exist heirloom varieties that may be worth considering.

Since our society worships youth, perhaps it is understandable that old seeds are often regarded as being in some manner inferior, outdated or not the trendy nineties kind of garden thing to sow. If most gardeners understood more about historic seeds, however, it would not take them long to comprehend the elements they are missing by not growing historic varieties.

Growing old seeds rarely means veering from your normal gardening regimen. If you are growing a historic bean, pea, tomato, potato or turnip, they will have the same requirements, for the most part, as the regular varieties. The only difference in making an assessment is that some of these historic varieties can help you grow better vegetables with more appeal and uses than conventional varieties.

Unfortunately, many varieties will exhibit different performance characteristics at different locations, even if these are located only a few feet from each other. Some of the elements that will effect the growth of a plant are: soil fertility and composition, slope, sun exposure, wind exposure, moisture and companion plants which may harbor pests or beneficial insects. Therefore, finding out if a historic variety is worthy to add to other annual gardening favorites usually means you will have to test them. For myself and many other gardeners, this is part of the fun. The other exciting feature is being able to grow the same vegetable that was grown and eaten generations ago. Many of the historic varieties are also visually interesting, for example striped tomatoes and artistically specked baking beans.

Basically, historic or heirloom seeds are the varieties which have survived the test of time, usually because they have been handed down from generation to generation. It is true that most of our vegetable seeds have undergone dramatic changes after decades and often centuries of breeding. In addition, just selecting the healthiest or best-looking vegetable for seeds naturally results in the healthiest and most desirable varieties for future generations.

It is also true that many of the older varieties are not nearly as attractive as some of the newer and better looking varieties. However, if you want flavor and don't care as much about how photogenic your produce is, many of the historic varieties could be an alternative, since many are packed full of flavor. I know what you're thinking: why don't many of the newer varieties have even better flavors? The answer is quite simple. Some do, but vegetables are bred to have a wide appeal, and anything that is distinct or particularly different in flavor is usually disregarded in favor of a selection with a more neutral flavor, the idea being that most people will like something that has nothing about it to dislike. The newer varieties are not void of flavor; it is just that in most cases, and in my own experience, many of the older varieties taste better than some of the newer hybrids.

There are also additional benefits to older varieties. Many of them are more disease-resistant, since they are closer to a wilder form. Many of them have superior keeping abilities, and some of them are early ripening and ideal for short seasons.

Saving Historic Seeds

Unfortunately, due to the scarcity and unavailability of some of the historic seeds, you may have to become a seed saver yourself in order to guarantee yourself a supply of your favorite varieties. This will not always be the case, since many seed companies do carry some of the older seeds, and they are usually designated in the catalogs as being a historic or heirloom variety.

Saving seeds can not only help guarantee survival for an heirloom variety, but can also save you a substantial amount of money. Let me explain. If you purchase a package of seeds for 95 cents plus taxes, and the package weighs 1/24 of an ounce, you are paying over $25.00 per pound for those seeds. It is not unusual to pay more for seeds on a per ounce basis than is paid for champagne, caviar, or even a new motor vehicle. Perhaps you can see why many large agribusinesses are also in the seed development business.

For the small grower, the savings can be substantial, especially if you use your own seeds and cuttings to start plants which you can sell. If you are gardening to any extent, you should be saving some of your own seeds. The savings can really add up, and you will have extra seeds to trade with neighbors and other gardeners.

Seed saving can be tricky, depending on variety. For instance, Swiss chard will cross-pollinate with beets, so you will have to save seeds during the alternating years when you grow these. Some varieties such as corn will have to be bagged, because they are not easily isolated. To do this, the immature ears are bagged to prevent foreign pollen from entering. When the pollen can be seen on the tassels, cut one off and rub it on the silk, (that's the material that's sticking out of the end of the ear) and then replace the bag. This will prevent the corn from being pollinated by a different variety. Of course, non-hybrid corn should be used, unless you want to create some new varieties.

I enjoy testing new varieties each year in the garden, and always include historic varieties. I have ended up growing many of these old varieties on a regular basis. Some of the varieties include Jacob's cattle bean, golden bantam corn (introduced in 1902), oakleaf lettuce (tolerates heat and resists bolting), yellow crookneck squash, as well as numerous unusual and novelty tomato varieties that I have tried over the last decade from the Tomato Seed Company. I will be trying some historic squash varieties this season. One particular variety was grown by the Indians in South Dakota, and is supposed to be able to keep for a full year when properly cured.

Historic seed varieties can add new flavors, textures and colors to your garden and meals. In addition, they can often provide you with a garden vegetable that you may have been unsuccessful in growing in the past because of susceptibility to disease, finicky requirements, or the fact that it was too early or too late to ripen. You will also be preserving and tasting a bit of history.

Plant Propagation

There are many excellent books and texts on the topic of plant propagation. I like to test all kinds of plant material that will grow in my area. Those plants which prove they can survive and produce acceptable harvests without succumbing to diseases and pests are candidates for propagation. For example, if I am growing an apple variety that I like, why would I pay fifteen dollars or more for a tree from a nursery when I can create one or even one hundred of my own for free? The same principle applies to other kinds of plant materials. Once you test a plant and are satisfied with it, you will probably want more of them. By knowing how to propagate your own plants you can create your own nursery stock, instead of paying others to propagate, grow, wholesale and retail the plant.

There are many different methods by which to propagate plants. Some plants are difficult, while others, such as raspberries and blackberries, will so quickly propagate themselves that they can take over your garden, given enough time.

This hardy kiwi from the former Soviet Union was started from a cutting. Today this plant produces an abundance of fruit.
(Martin P. Waterman photo.)

When planning your self-sufficiency garden, you should consider which plants are easily propagated. You should also have an understanding of the different propagation methods and which are best for the plants that you want to grow.

Propagation Techniques

Cuttings are a popular method of propagation. Sometimes, rooting hormones need to be used, and in some cases, a greenhouse type environment is necessary. This does not mean you necessarily need a greenhouse. I often start cuttings in old milk cartons and simply cover the carton with a plastic bag held in place with an elastic band to create the proper environment. Different parts of a plant can be used, such as stems, leaves or root pieces, depending on the plant.

Tomatoes are one of the most versatile and popular of gardening plants. Few people realize that they can also be propagated by cuttings.
(Martin P. Waterman photo.)

Division is another method of propagation that's ideally suited for certain types of plants. This usually entails digging up the plant and cutting it in two pieces or more by dividing its root mass and top growth into two or more separate smaller plants. I am continually dividing my chives, horseradish and rhubarb plants to make new plants. As it turns out, this is a sensible practice, since older plants become less productive. Once divided, they become rejuvenated.

Layering is one of the best ways to propagate certain plants, since it is easy and requires little in the way of time or tools. For instance, if you bend a raspberry or currant cane so that you can bury a section under the soil, that part of the plant will form roots and can later be removed as a new plant. This process often happens naturally in certain plant varieties.

Grafting is another type of propagation. Many gardeners will grow their own apple rootstocks and then graft the varieties they want onto them. Grafting can be a lot of fun, since it allows you to try a wide range of material in a small space. I have heard of as many as 500 different apple varieties being grafted onto a single tree. While this may be a little unrealistic (especially keeping track of what is growing on which branch), grafting will allow you to try a large variety of plant material to see which are suited to your climate, your personal tastes or your commercial marketing plans.

I cannot over emphasize the importance of seed saving and propagation, especially if self-sufficiency is your goal. After you have to pay for a few seed and plant orders, you may begin to see what I mean by the substantial cash savings that can be realized.

Recommended Reading

Foolproof Planting: How to Successfully Start and Propagate More Than 250 Vegetables, Trees and Shrubs by Anne Moyer Halpin and the editors of Rodale Press. Rodale Press Inc., 1990. ISBN 0-87857-944-X. This books takes hundreds of the most popular plants and shows you how best to grow them, as well as how to propagate them.

Saving Seeds: The Gardener's Guide to Growing and Storing Vegetable and Flower Seeds by Marc Rogers. Storey Communications, Inc., 1992. ISBN 0-88266-634-7. Highly recommended book that will show you how to save seeds and a substantial amount of money from your garden.

Secrets of Plant Propagation: Starting Your Own Flowers, Vegetables, Fruits, Berries, Shrubs, Trees and Houseplants by Lewis Hill. Storey Communications, Inc., 1985. ISBN 0-88266-370-4. A useful reference book on how to propagate a large selection of plant material.

Chapter Twelve

Preserving and Storing Your Crops

There is little point in growing food, only to have the use of it for just a short period of time, or having much of it die on the vine or perish in storage. A system to preserve and store your crops is crucial in order to guarantee yourself a safe and nutritious supply of food for the long haul.

It is unfortunate that many people have the perception that food that is stored for long periods of time must be dull and tasteless. When most people think of food for storage, they often think of military, camping and survival type food.

The fact of the matter is that by growing and creating your own food for long-term storage, you can make it as fancy and delicious as you want. A trip to your local supermarket will quickly demonstrate that not only can everyday foods be stored for long periods of time, but so can all types of gourmet foods. In fact, much of the canned food on your local grocery store's shelves may have been there for a very long time. Storage of foods does not always have to mean diminishing quality. Certain foods will actually improve in quality over the long term.

Keep in mind that if your objective is to put away a large volume of food, this will take time and energy. How *much* time and energy will depend on the type of food you plan to preserve and the manner in which you intend to preserve it.

If you just want to store potatoes, beets and carrots in the root cellar and a few hundred pounds of dried beans in containers, your work will be relatively straightforward. If you plan on canning and bottling your own tomatoes, ketchup and chili, be prepared to spend some time in the kitchen.

I have found that there are certain tricks to putting away the harvest. One is not to wait until the end of the growing season. If you do wait until the end of the growing season to can your tomatoes, the task could be overwhelming. If you do a batch every two weeks or so, however, by the end of the season, you can have much of your work already completed. There is a good argument for growing a wide variety of foods so that they do not become ripe and ready for preserving all at once. During the growing season, I usually spend a part of my Sundays doing my cooking and preserving. By the time the snow begins to fall in late autumn, practically all of my work is done.

When preserving food, it helps to have the right equipment on hand, such as canning jars, lids and a large pot or pressure cooker. The cost of this equipment can be high the first year when you are putting a lot of food away, but the jars and equipment are reusable, and thus the following year the costs will be minimal.

It is amazing how much food you can put away in one day if you plan correctly. Another thing I find that is very beneficial is to do my preserving with a friend. One person can be peeling or cooking and slicing, while the other is preparing and filling the jars. If you can with other people, you can also trade some of your finished product for a greater selection of food than might otherwise be available.

There are many factors to consider when planning the food that you wish to preserve. These factors will help you to quickly design a game plan that will be consistent with your objectives. This in turn will help you to structure the kind of food you want to grow, since you will have a defined understanding of what to do when you bring in the harvest.

Refrigeration and Freezing

I love freezing food. I freeze hundreds of pounds of tomatoes, beans, broccoli, strawberries, blueberries, rhubarb and other produce. But I am painfully aware of what would happen if I were to lose electricity for any length of time. Because of that possibility, I also use several other methods to preserve my crops, and have contingency plans should the freezer have a seizure.

Even if you have an alternative energy source such as a gas generator or solar power, the amount of food a deep freeze can hold is limited. There is nothing wrong with having the deep freeze full, but it should not contain the sum and substance of your food storage inventory.

Freezers and refrigerators can play an important role for those who harvest a substantial amount of food, yet have limited time for preservation. In the summer and autumn I freeze a lot of raspberries and strawberries. In the winter, when I am obviously not busy in the garden, I can then make jam and other preserves from this fruit. If you are short of time or must be away from your produce at harvest time, you can temporarily freeze or refrigerate all kinds of produce and then use other preparation and preservation methods at your convenience.

Time

As mentioned earlier, it will take some time to preserve your harvest. You need to study the preservation options that are available. It is a good idea to investigate by reading some books on canning and preserving. Many cookbooks have entire sections devoted to various preserving recipes.

This is an important thing to consider, since once you expose yourself to different options and opportunities, your preferred manner of storing a food or food product could be changed. For instance, I used to store the majority of my beans by simply drying them. I still do this, but I have also found that the young string beans taste excellent if they are preserved with pickling spices, garlic and a little hot pepper. As I mentioned earlier, preserved foods need not be boring.

The point of the matter is that pickling takes more time than drying, drying requires more time than canning and canning uses up more time than freezing.

Your time is a valuable resource, and it will have to be budgeted in such a way that you get the results you are seeking from your preservation program.

These beans are being dried efficiently and inexpensively by the sun.
(Martin P. Waterman photo.)

Where Are You Going to Put All the Stuff?

Space is often a consideration for many of us. For instance, 200 pounds of dry beans does not take much room, but 400 jars with a half a pound of beans in each can take up a considerable amount of room.

If you plan to have a large harvest, you may have to build yourself a cold room or root cellar. Many gardening books have plans for these structures. There are also books totally devoted to storing your fruits and vegetables.

When you plan your garden, preservation methods should be in the back of your mind. Each year when I plan my garden, I do so with the knowledge of how much food I preserved from last season and which foods kept the best and tasted good. Food preservation is an ever evolving process that changes with the type of harvest, available time, food preferences and cravings. I find that each year my preserved food improves in quality and quantity, and I am continually increasing the number of methods which I use to preserve. I am also expanding the areas in which I store my preserved food.

Dinner for How Many?

Although my inventory fluctuates, I like to have enough food on hand to last about a year. If you want more than a year's worth of food, it's not hard to up your production.

From a financial standpoint, it makes good sense to have enough food on hand so that you do not have to purchase fruit and vegetables when they are selling at a premium price. If you froze or canned tomatoes during the summer when they were about half a dollar per pound, you will be glad you did so in the winter when they can be many times as expensive. In some cases, tomatoes can even be more expensive than some of the better cuts of chicken and beef.

How many people do you want to feed, and for how long? This is a question you should ask yourself if your objective is a safe and inexpensive food supply to sustain you, regardless of the conditions around you.

Nutrition and a Balanced Diet

When preserving your foods, remember that certain preservation methods do a better job of protecting the nutritional value of your food than others. Try to preserve foods in such a manner that you have a representation of all the major food groups, so you continually have a healthy and balanced diet. Fruits and vegetables may be lacking in certain important elements such as protein. Do not forget that you can also preserve beef, poultry and other meats. These foods can be preserved as is or used in recipes that can be canned or preserved in different forms. If you have any livestock, you may want to think about a smokehouse so that you can preserve your own meats.

Don't forget medicinal foods or those foods that have the ability to act as medicines. Many gardeners keep a herbal medicine chest, as well as making sure that the healing and healthful herbs are used amply in much of their preserved foods.

Of course, if you preserve your own foods, you have control over the type of preservatives that you are using. Many consumers have a distrust of commercial products, since they have very little understanding of the types or consequences of ingesting large amounts of preservatives. Many preservatives in commercial foods have little to do with shelf life, as they simply act to make the food look more attractive in a supermarket environment where it will be exposed to heat, light and movement.

Safety Considerations

Certain preservation methods are safer than others. Botulism can be a problem when canning foods and not following directions pertaining to proper temperatures and sanitation. Practically any book on preservation will have information about how to avoid situations where food poisoning can occur. As long as you follow directions, you should have no cause for worry. If some food does go bad, it will usually be very apparent by visual inspection or simply smelling it.

Rotate Your Food

To protect the integrity of the food that you have in storage, don't forget to use the oldest foods first and the newly preserved foods last. You will also need to have an understanding of which types of preserved foods have the longest shelf lives and which ones don't. By knowing this, you can manage your stored harvest so that there should be very little waste or spoilage.

Best Methods

The best methods are the ones that will work best for you and suit your short-term and long-term food needs. You will also want to consider which foods taste best when preserved by using different preservation methods and recipes. Personally, I can't seem to put away enough pickled beets. To me, pickled beets are like candy. Dried apples made into fruit leather is another favorite. These go very well chopped up in cereal or used to make a high-energy trail mix.

When I first started to preserve food, most of the food that I preserved was on the boring side. I was trying to duplicate dehydrated camping type food. Today, the food that I preserve, in all modesty, is gourmet, and is superior to most foods you can purchase at your grocery store. I find that I am making all kinds of condiments such as hot pepper jams, mint sauce, and all sorts of hot sauces. I am also experimenting with many preservation methods, including sun drying and candy making.

There are many commercial products available now to dry and dehydrate food, and they are worth investigating. You may feel that some of these products are over priced, and lots of them are. Keep searching, for there are some very good products available at reasonable prices. Remember, for your canning and preserving equipment, you want something that is going to last for a long time. Good equipment will usually come with a dependable and long warranty or guarantee.

Food dryers and dehydrators can often be made quite economically, and some food can even be dried in your oven using low heat, even though this can be more costly than other methods. If your climate permits, certain foods can be dried or cured by the sun. There are also solar food dryers and dehydrators that can be built or purchased.

You don't have to have a garden to start practicing and experimenting with preserving. Food preservation is a very important skill for self preservation, and can be an enjoyable way to enhance your meals and your quality of life.

Recommended Reading

Keeping the Harvest: Preserving Your Fruits, Vegetables and Herbs by Nancy Chioffi & Gretchen Mead. Storey Communications, Inc., 1992. ISBN 0-88266-650-9. This book will show you a wide range of preserving techniques, including freezing, canning, pressure canning, drying, pickling, curing and making jams and jellies. A very thorough book.

The Harvest Gardener: Growing for Maximum Yield, Prime Flavor, and Garden Fresh Storage by Susan McClure. Storey Communications, Inc., 1993. ISBN 0-88266-797-1. This book will help you structure your garden and resulting harvest with the objective of putting away the best quality and quantity of food.

Root Cellaring: Natural Cold Storage of Fruits & Vegetables by Mike and Nancy Bubel. Storey Communications, Inc. ISBN 0-88266-703-3. 1991. Learn the age-old, low-cost ways to create natural storage systems for nearly 100 crops, plus how to choose the foods that will store best.

Country Wines: Making & Using Wines from Herbs, Fruits, Flowers & More by Pattie Vargas and Rich Gulling. Storey Communications, Inc., 1991. ISBN 0-88266-749-1. Learn to make wine from wheat, parsley, dandelions, raspberries, peaches and other crops that you can grow.

Chapter Thirteen

Earning Income with Your Crops

There are many ways to earn money with your crops, so in this chapter I will introduce a few models that can easily be adopted. As is the case with any type of business, it is wise to study successful operations and strive to duplicate the things they are doing correctly. You can also analyze their weaknesses; in other words, it is usually far better to learn from other people's mistakes than to make your own. In studying what people are doing in your particular area, you may be able to identify niche or new markets that are not being exploited.

There are some basic rules to follow when your objective is to sell some of the crops which you have grown. First and foremost, no matter which course you take to market your produce or value-added products, it is highly recommended that you test the market before you mortgage the house or bet the farm on your new enterprise.

The second rule is to start small so that you can afford to make numerous mistakes and miscalculations. Then, if and when these errors occur, the results will not put your security in jeopardy. Of course, one of the advantages of self-sufficiency gardening as a route to financial and other security is that you can start as small as you like and then grow without making a major investment. I know of one landscaper who had a rather large garden. He used it to earn about $4,000 to $5,000 per year, just by selling fresh produce to friends, neighbors and customers. Over time, he learned their needs and grew the produce his customers wanted. When you consider his extra income and the amount of money he saved on his annual food bill, you can see there is practically enough money produced to pay the mortgage on a house, or provide a sizable amount of money to invest each and every year. He does this with little effort, and he considers his small garden to be a hobby and pure enjoyment.

If you plan on selling produce, one of the most important things that you can do is to know your market. If you have Italians in your area, for instance, you may be able to sell a great deal of herb basil and paste tomatoes. Hispanics and other nationalities love hot peppers. These are generalities, but the point is that there are people out there who will give you cash if you grow the vegetables that they like and for which they are constantly searching.

When selling your produce, you can also start small and test the market, and this should not in any manner be a difficult undertaking. It is not like brain surgery or landing a spacecraft on Mars. Mistakes are not fatal; all you are doing is selling some excess produce or taking your produce and seeing if the market justifies your planting and harvesting more.

The best way to test your market is to simply bring fresh produce to your local grocer, farmers' market, convenience store, health food store or restaurant. Many of these businesses love to purchase fresh local produce. What is more important is that they will probably not hesitate to tell you exactly the items they need, when they need them, and how much they are willing to pay for them. It won't take long until you have an understanding of your local market, and once you discover a niche market, you could be in business more quickly than you think. A produce buyer at a large local supermarket was not shy in telling me that he has difficulty getting enough acorn squash, particularly some of the newer varieties. Fresh peas were another type of produce that never seemed to last long in his produce section.

If you can find several vendors for a given produce item, you are likely to be able to sell it all and choose the vendors with whom you most enjoy working. Hopefully, these will also be the vendors who offer the best price and most prompt payment.

If you find that you have difficulty meeting the demands of local vendors for fresh produce, you can even become an agent or distributor for other growers, and get a commission for selling their produce. You could also find yourself in the produce wholesale business, especially if you are aggressive at marketing and can get a good price for your produce.

By having contacts made before you grow a certain food, you very likely will be able to sell it at a premium price. If you cannot sell certain produce, there are alternatives. You could lower your prices, or you could still put this produce away for your own use. This is one of the reasons that most of the produce I grow just happens to be produce that is easily preserved.

Don't be afraid to talk to your local grocery stores. I have even found out a lot of information that I needed over the telephone. It is best to go and visit some produce managers in person, however. You may be surprised with the results, especially if you bring them fresh fruits and herbs.

Every produce manager I talked with had a list of fresh fruits and vegetables that they wanted to purchase locally. Certain crops such as raspberries have a very short shelf life. Crops such as these, which are rarely seen in grocery stores, could be a sensible choice. I found that they were in demand from many grocery stores. Of course, raspberries can be labor intensive to pick, but this book presupposes that the reader does not expect the government or others to pay his way or take care of him in life.

There is also a growing demand for exotic foods. You can experiment with many unique crops in your area, such as mushrooms, different types of herbs and spices, Chinese vegetables and other specialty foods. If you keep your costs under control, your risk will be minimized, and any leftover or unsold produce can be consumed or preserved for your own use or later resale.

Restaurants can be a gold mine. I know a grower who, among his many crops, grows asparagus and garlic. He took fresh produce and simply left a giant heap of it for the chef to sample and try. He went back to see the chef, and now he provides the restaurant with much of their fresh produce. You would be surprised how much fresh fruit and vegetables a restaurant can use, particularly if you find a chef with whom you can develop a good working relationship. If you have good produce at competitive prices, a chef will often highlight your products in daily specials and use them in numerous recipes. Fresh produce has a taste and texture different from something that has been in a food broker's warehouse for a few weeks, and customers will pay a premium price for it, or at the very least will patronize the restaurant again and again.

Senior citizens are another hot market for fresh produce, since many of them grew up in rural areas. Place some notices in or near senior citizens' homes or areas where these people live. Senior citizens have a disproportionately high percentage of the nation's wealth, and therefore money to spend. Many do not like to go out too often. It is a scary world for many of them, because they are often the target of crime. You may want to recruit your local paperboy or another youngster to make deliveries. You will not have to pay him much, and he may even earn extra money in tips. You may also be able to pay him to harvest produce as well. Seniors are a great market for value-added products such as jams and jellies. Don't forget to send your best customers Christmas or even birthday cards. You are in business, and if you keep your customers happy, they will keep you happy.

I have sold to farmers' markets, but then I was taking a discount for my produce. For example, I can sell all the grapes I can grow to farmers' markets for a dollar a pound. They, in turn, sell them for two to three dollars a pound. Now I sell direct to people, many of whom come back year after year, for a couple of dollars a pound. Believe me, it makes a big difference when you can sell direct and cut out any middlemen. If you can make an extra 50 cents a pound on your produce by selling direct to the consumer, and you sell a measly 3,000 pounds during the season, you will have earned an *additional* fifteen hundred dollars.

Speaking of money, if you have built yourself a root cellar, cold room or a structure to store your own vegetables, you can extend your selling season. If you are selling squash for a couple of bucks apiece in August, the same squash may command four to five dollars at Christmas time. If you plan on selling much of your produce, consider the value of extending your selling season and cash flow. It may even be advisable for you not to not sell certain crops such as cabbage when the prices are low, but instead begin to market the cabbage when the prices rise during the winter months.

U-Pick Operations

One of the most simple and basic operations is a U-Pick farm. This can include growing almost anything from strawberries and raspberries to citrus and other fruits and vegetables. When done correctly, a U-Pick operation can be very profitable.

There is a large constituency of people who enjoy the thrill of picking their own produce, especially if they are from larger urban areas. You would be surprised how far people will travel for fresh produce, particularly if you are offering something special, such as organically grown produce.

If you are planning a U-pick operation, you will need to advertise your presence at first. You can place classified ads in your local and surrounding newspapers. Many consumers are very receptive to foods which are free of chemical residues, particularly if they suffer from a poor immune system or a distrust of modern food production systems. Their only motive may be common sense, but whatever the reason, they are customers who would be willing to make a special trip to harvest from your fields.

Strawberries are one of the most popular U-pick crops.
(U.S.D.A. photo.)

Of course, one of the big advantages of a U-pick operation is that you no longer have the expense of harvesting. You will probably have to till more often,

since the soil will tend to get compacted from the increased traffic, but the profits will far outweigh any expenses.

You, or someone you trust, will also have to be present during harvest, since these operations can generate a lot of cash in a short time.

Location is very important for these types of operations. If you have access to a busy road, you will be able to attract more customers. Many U-pick operators will build a small market or structure to sell already harvested produce, plus some value-added products. Many will also sell crafts from local artists, as well as other groceries. The possibilities are many, but the standard rule of thumb is to start small.

Another key to success in a U-pick operation is to grow the several types of crops with the widest appeal. Customers will travel far and wide to pick strawberries and raspberries, but are unlikely to have the same motivation for rutabagas and kohlrabi. If your U-pick does have several appealing crops, you will not be vulnerable if you have some crop failures. A study of your market and prices will soon tell you which are the most lucrative crops to grow. I know a fruit breeder in New England who put his children through college from the income from a four-acre U-pick blueberry operation. They come from far and wide and line up during the picking season; for many of the customers, it has become an annual tradition.

Rent a Garden

Here is an interesting way to make money, particularly if you are not far from a large urban area. Take a piece of land and divide it into plots of about 20 by 20 feet, allowing for a wide path in between. Rent these plots to gardeners who live in the city, but, because they are apartment or condo dwellers, have no garden. They get more than a garden. They get a place in the country to visit on weekends and evenings, and the pleasure of growing their own food. Many operations such as these have been very successful. Rent 100 spaces at $50 per space, and you can probably pay for the land during your first year. You can have different plots of different sizes, and you can even make extra money by selling bedding plants and seeds. You can also rent them your tiller and other equipment.

If you are just starting out, you can rent or option a piece of land and try it for one year. You can then use this land for your own gardening trials, and sublet the excess land to others. If your enterprise proves successful and encouraging, you can then purchase the land.

*You may want to try growing flowers such
as these Verbena. You may be surprised
at how many you are able to sell.*
(All-America Selections photo.)

Your Own Farmers' Market

If you live in a town with a number of vacant properties, you may be able to rent one during the growing season. An old closed down gas station can come alive as a fresh produce stand.

In a nearby town with a population of about 1,500 people, some small growers rented a small, older building and opened a produce stand. At the beginning, 90% of their produce was purchased from a large produce wholesaler. Nonetheless, it established them in business and allowed them to have an outlet for their own produce. They also purchase produce from other gardeners and farmers in the area, including myself. Their business is booming, so much so that they added more groceries and now sell bedding plants during the season. This year they will not be renting, but instead will have a building of their own.

They started small, as a seasonal operation, and now have a successful business. Since they now sell many of their own crops, they are making a retail, wholesale and farming profit.

Someone Else's Farmers' Market

If you don't want to sell at your own farmers' market, there may be some flea markets or other farmers' markets in your area that rent booth space. Often a table at one of these markets is very reasonable, costing as little a $20 for the day. You can often recoup this cost in minutes, and this is an ideal way to start marketing your crops.

If there are no such farmers' markets or flea markets in your area, contact the management of your local arena, drive-in movie or similar space, and find out how much it costs to rent. You may find that you can soon have your own flea market or farmers' market where you can rent booths to others. In one town near my home, the local farmers' market is in the basement of a service club. Every Friday night and Saturday, about 30 merchants sell everything from candles, sausages, breads, preserves and crafts to fresh produce. It is a very successful operation, and a popular destination.

Vacant Lots and Travel

Another grower I know has a very simple and proven way to market his produce. He loads up his van until it almost bursts on a Saturday or Sunday morning. He drives to town and sets up on a vacant corner or lot. Usually, he will have sold all his produce by noon, and can often repeat this more than once each day. There is no shortage of vacant lots or spaces where this can be done.

I once met a man and woman who had a farmers' market in a small town in Texas. They purchased much of their produce locally, but the man would drive a 2-ton truck to California every week to purchase directly from farmers there. I asked him if it paid him to do so, and when I heard the figures, I could hardly believe the additional money he earned with each trip. If your market will not come to you, consider going to your market.

Sell Bedding Plants and Flowers and Container Plants

This market can become competitive, but there is money to be made. A very important niche seems to be the marketing of container plants. These have appeal for those who live on small lots or in apartments, but who would like to have some fresh produce or herbs. Potted flowers and roses are also popular, as are window boxes that are preplanted.

Container plants are very popular especially in urban areas with small lots and balcony gardeners.
(All-American Selections photo.)

Container plants are one of the fastest growth areas for garden centers and plant retailers. This market recognizes that plant breeders, scientists and seed companies are creating more plants which feature dwarf and miniature habits that are ideal for pot culture. What is even more surprising is that many of these plants do not short-change you on producing regular size crops.

Many of the most popular vegetables are ideal for container culture. When this is the case, or if a plant has a dwarf habit that lends itself to container culture, it will usually be noted in seed catalogs.

Tomatoes are one of the most popular container or patio plants. A good variety is Husky Gold Tomato, which is a dwarf indeterminate plant, which makes it ideal for container planting. The plants are compact, and are heavy producers of tasty fruits that average about 8 ounces. The plant should not grow higher than three feet, and fruit should be ready about 68 days after transplanting.

If I could recommend one new tomato for everyone to try, it would have to be Sweet Million, which is an improved version of Sweet 100. I have had as many as 300 cherry tomatoes from one of these plants. Gardeners with longer seasons (mine averages only about 125 days) have reported yields of over 500 tomatoes. If you remove the suckers and train two stems, these plants will grow over six feet in a season.

The best part is that these tomatoes are sweet and tasty, so much so that I have heard them referred to as candy tomatoes. If this name is not because of their sweetness, then it is because they are eaten as quickly as candy.

Another popular container crop is cucumbers, and many of these are available in bush habits. A few well-fed plants can usually give you all the cucumbers you may require during the season, plus a few extra to use in making pickles.

Another popular container plant is peppers. They seem to be the perfect size to be grown in a container. Many chefs, amateur and professional, cannot live without their container gardens full of fresh herbs such as basil, rosemary, mint and thyme. Many people who like herbal teas grow their own herbs in containers to give them a supply of fresh material for their favorite hot beverages and mixtures.

Container gardening is relatively new, and you may have to educate your customers. Once embarked, they may become loyal, and could come back every year, especially when they see that the tomato plant you sold them gave them an endless supply of tomatoes. Container plants are best when started very early in the season, since they will sell quickly and for a premium price if there is fruit already on them. I have seen bearing tomato plants sell for as much as $12. You can buy large fibre pot containers or large plastic containers from the wholesalers listed in the back of landscape magazines, or in your Yellow Pages.

Starting your own plants from seeds is a very simple process.
(National Garden Bureau photo.)

Another important benefit derived from container gardening is that your customers can prolong their growing season. If it looks as if there will be a frost or bad weather, they simply bring the plants inside for the night or place garbage bags over them to protect them.

Many gardeners in cold climates grow dwarf peach, cherry and fig trees in containers. Since these would not have a chance of survival upon being exposed during a cold winter, in the autumn they are placed in a sheltered area such as a cellar or unheated garage or building. When the warmer temperatures return in the spring, the containers can be moved outdoors. There is a good market for these types of plants as well.

You may also want to consider the art of growing bonsai plants, dwarf ornamentals or other flowering plants. Specialize and try to offer items that no one else is exploiting.

Value-Added Food Products

The appeal of value-added products is that there is more money to be made with them than in selling the raw product. A farmer gets but a few pennies of the several dollars that a box of cereal sells for at a supermarket.

Value-added products can be tricky, and "caution" is the key word. The secret of success is to have a product of such uniqueness or high quality that you will stand out and gain a following. Many people try to sell their own homemade jams, salsas, pickles and similar items. If you can sell a bushel of cucumbers and earn $10, it may be wiser to turn them into pickles and sell the same amount for many times that figure. You will also have to consider your canning equipment and time. You may find that you are only earning a few dollars per hour. On the other hand, you could be earning a premium wage and may be in a position to hire more people.

Value-added products can take some time and effort to launch, so remember not to invest your entire harvest in these types of enterprises.

An interesting and often profitable way to sell value-added products is the catering business. You may already have much of the food needed for a good start in this enterprise. If you cater a wedding, birthday or other celebration, it is not unusual to command $5 to $10 per person, depending on the menu. For feeding 100 people, your total food bill can be kept under several hundred dollars, and you can feed them lavishly. If you are only moderately

successful, and in the course of one year can only do ten jobs in which you earn $500, that is an extra $5,000 per year. This figure may not even include the additional money saved, in effect, by purchasing food from yourself. Many caterers can earn over one hundred thousand dollars per year once established. Don't forget to include caterers on your list of possible purchasers of your produce when looking for markets.

Farm-Related Products

When considering money making possibilities, try not to limit your thinking. For example, in my area we have many German immigrants. One particular family of German descent started out raising bees in order to have honey to sell. Bees were a natural choice since they pollinate the crops in our area. They are also able to sell candles which they make from the wax, and even export these candles and other wax products.

Value-Added Craft Supplies

Your garden can be a valuable source of materials with which to make crafts or other products. There are many books available on this topic. It can be a risky business in the beginning, but you do not have to put all your eggs in one basket. Start with a few samples, and then you could be well on your own way. If you think you have a good product, investigate renting a booth at a flea market or farmers' market. If you receive some interest, investigate some of the many craft shows, especially the ones held before Christmas time. Also, visit local craft shops and see what they are purchasing. Many in this area will purchase grape vines or evergreen tips for use as Christmas wreaths and other crafts.

Saving Money with Your Crops

For Christmas gifts one year, I gave hastily made wooden boxes containing 4 or 5 of my jams (including my famous pumpkin-orange and strawberry-rhubarb). I have never received so much praise for Christmas gifts. They were very inexpensive to make, and I still get requests for them. Your crafts, foods and other garden products have great value, and sharing them with friends, family and associates can be an extremely rewarding experience. If you are in business, it is a wise practice to butter up your customers with a Christmas present or some type of remembrance, so that you will be first and foremost in their mind.

Barter

Don't forget that you can also trade food for other services and goods. If you trade $100 worth of food (that may have cost you literally pennies to produce) for some beef, poultry, electrical work or anything else, you have saved yourself money, and have, in effect, earned yourself money.

There are many ways to earn money with your crops, and no doubt you will probably discover some on your own. Don't forget that the objective is financial, physical and emotional security through home food and related production.

Recommended Reading

The Potential of Herbs as a Cash Crop by Richard Alan Miller. Acres, USA, 1985. ISBN 0-911311-10-6. The nuts and bolts of creating a small herb farm and marketing your products. 230 pages of highly useful information.

Growing Your Herb Business by Bertha Reppert. Storey Communications, Inc., 1994. ISBN 0-88266-612-6. The author has had an herb and spice business for over 25 years and she shares her own experience and the experience of 50 other herb business owners.

Secrets to a Successful Greenhouse Business: A Complete Guide to Starting and Operating A High Profit Business That's Beneficial to the Environment by T.M Taylor, Box 243, Melbourne, Florida 32902, 1991. ISBN 0-9628678-0-2. How to grow cash crops fast with your greenhouse, and where to market them. Easy-to-follow and solid advice, plus greenhouse plans.

Shadow Merchants: Successful Retailing without a Store Front by Jordan L. Cooper. Loompanics Unlimited, 1993. ISBN 1-55950-105-7. This book will explain how to sell your goods without a store front. Includes secrets of selling at swap meets, flea markets, street kiosks and even carnivals.

Chapter Fourteen

The Future of Sustainable Agriculture

It often comes as a great surprise to many people that the largest industry in the United States is not electronics or automobiles, tourism or travel; it is agriculture.

With modern technology continuing to change agricultural production methods, there is concern over the future of sustainable agriculture. One of the most serious concerns is whether or not the small grower or farmer will be able to survive and compete against large mechanized agribusinesses. The small grower also has to contend with lower priced imported commodities, along with increased production costs and regulations.

To understand the future of agriculture, we need only look at how our modern-day agricultural systems developed. To do this, we first must understand the past.

The history of agriculture is inseparable from the history of mankind. Agriculture enabled man to have a reliable food supply, which in turn encouraged permanent settlements. This led to the subsequent development of civilizations. Before this, man was nomadic and hunted, which usually meant that he was forced to follow the food supply.

The dawn of agriculture probably began with the cultivation of wild rice, wheat and corn. The earliest dates to which scientists attribute the start of agriculture were during the Middle Stone Age, which occurred as late as 8,000 to 6,500 BC. It was during this time that man began to sow seeds and keep animals. Dogs were some of the first of the animals to be tamed, and were usually used for hunting. It is likely that man was gathering and planting seeds long before that time.

Agriculture evolved very slowly over a period of thousands of years, and some cultures today continue practices that date back 10,000 years or more. This is an important fact to remember. With the explosion of scientific breakthroughs that provide us with so many conveniences, it should be noted that some seeds, soil, sun and water are all that is needed to grow many types of the food which we find necessary to sustain us. Always keep in mind that food production is, at its core, a very simple process which even the most primitive cultures have been able to master.

The agricultural revolution can be traced to Britain during the late 18th century, even though it may have actually started somewhat earlier. The British were responsible for several innovations. This included the use of plants which added nitrogen to the soil, and the practice of crop rotation. When livestock crops were grown, the manure would improve the soil so that it could be used almost immediately for a new crop. This enabled infertile land to become productive quickly. There are many nitrogen fixing crops which can be grown to improve your own soil's fertility.

In the early 19th century, the steam plow, the mechanical threshing machine and drill planters did even more to improve the state of agriculture. Today's grower has a multitude of types of garden equipment from which to choose, allowing him to function on any level. From small garden tillers to large tractors, equipment is such that food production can be done on any scale. At the other end of the equation, horses are still being used effectively, and this method of agricultural development is gaining more and more converts.

Failures of Modern Agriculture

There are many failures in agriculture, and most of these are economic failures and not failures of the land to produce a crop. Many farmers are trapped in a system of farming which requires them to produce a commodity that costs them more to grow than they receive for selling it. Governments encourage the farmers to grow these crops, and often subsidize them, since most farm lobbies are a powerful political force. Throughout history, landholders have usually had a large degree of power, and unless they abdicate their control to bankers or governments that strip them of their property rights, they usually remain a powerful political and economic force.

Poor farming practices have resulted in erosion, which has left some of the most fertile land in North America unable to support a crop. Over-reliance on chemical herbicides, fungicides and other chemicals has left soil dead, and limited the benefits of important microorganisms. Much land that has been used for agriculture has been abandoned or allowed to become overgrown, since it no longer has a useful purpose. When there is a lack of respect for the land, eventually it will result in diminished harvests.

Your Key to Success

There are many things that you can do to ensure that you can sustain your food production and livelihood. If you grow a multiplicity of crops you will be protected if there happens to be disease, insect infestations, drought or any other problem that can cause crop failure. If you have planned your "grub stake" appropriately, you should be able to at least supplement your income for years. It is rare that there is a 100% crop failure, and if you have put food away during the good years, you can absorb the losses during the poor years. If your program includes greenhouses or indoor hydroponics, you should always have fresh food on hand throughout the year. Conventional agriculture still relies on weather, and the weather, especially as of late, can be very unpredictable.

If you practice composting and continually add organic material to your soil, you will find that by looking after your land, no matter how small, it will also look after you.

Some Thoughts about the Future

Today, agriculture is going through another revolution, and that is the technological revolution. Gene transfer and similar technologies are permitting the creation of designer plants. One example of gene transfer concerns some mosses that are common to the West. After severe drought, the dried out plant will turn a lush green in as little as 30 seconds after water is applied. The cells undergo a miraculous healing in a matter of minutes. Scientists are mapping the genes responsible for this transformation, and once isolated, these same genes will be transferred to different species of grasses to create new varieties. These new varieties are being developed for livestock feed that can tolerate drought and stress, and then still recover from the most difficult conditions that nature can provide.

Gene transfer has already produced plants which will resist diseases and pests, and has created new varieties that will make agriculture more efficient.

Agriculture will probably undergo more changes in the next 50 years than it did in the last 5,000. There are many challenges ahead. With so few varieties of grain crops such as corn being grown, there are fears that a single disease could wreak havoc if allowed to get a foothold.

This happened in 1970, when a disease called Southern corn leaf blight destroyed 15% of the corn crop in the U.S. (almost a billion bushels). Because of this vulnerability, governments and private organizations are now trying to preserve the seeds of the vast varieties of fruit, vegetables and grains before they are lost.

All change brings with it a measure of controversy. Some of the changes that affect plant material have brought an extra degree of controversy, especially since so many health concerns have been suggested. What makes genetic engineering particularly controversial is that it deals with the realm of the unknown, which is something that most people fear. There is still little known about the effects of genetic engineering and how it may ultimately effect those who consume the product.

In conducting my research, I was surprised to find the number of potential dangers that have been cited. The improvements attributed to genetic engineering hold great promise, as they can ensure a more reliable food supply produced with less effort. But the potential downside of this practice also needs to be examined. I will mention some of the major concerns, but remember that these do not, by any measure, represent all the concerns that have been expressed.

One of the most controversial factors is that new toxicants could be added to genetically engineered food. There are many plants which contain compounds that are toxic to humans. Three toxins that are present in existing foods are neurotoxins, enzyme inhibitors and hemolytic substances. Although these are regularly consumed, they do not exist at toxic levels. The FDA has noted, however, that genetically engineered food could result in these toxins being produced at higher levels.

Genetic engineering could also change the metabolic pathways of plants. Mutations can render the metabolic pathways of plants inoperable, or activate pathways that have ceased to function during the plant's evolution. There is a concern that genetic engineering may reactivate such pathways. Toxicants which have never been associated with the plant may now be produced.

Genetic engineered foods could also interfere with some prescription drugs. Many people rely on antibiotics. Genetically altered foods contain antibiotic-resistant genes that may diminish the effectiveness of some antibiotics in both humans and domestic animals. Antibiotic genes are regularly incorporated into genetically engineered organisms as markers. The primary function of these markers is to tell the scientists if the organism has been successfully engineered. The FDA has stated that antibiotic-resistant genes and their enzyme products are expected to be present in foods derived from engineered plants. The possibility exists that these genes will produce enzymes which can inactivate antibiotics, and thus reduce the effectiveness of the medicine.

The most frightening effects are those that are unseen and undetectable. Most people like to eat a tomato when they buy a tomato. But, scientists have already introduced new proteins that differ significantly in structure from those that existed before the plant was altered. In addition, carbohydrates, fats and oils could be changed, which in turn could dramatically change the plant material or fruit that is being altered. So the effect could be that the fruit or vegetable that you eat could be very much different chemically from the ones you are used to eating. There is also a concern over counterfeit freshness. Traits can be introduced that will give a fruit or vegetable the appearance that it is fresh, when in truth it could be spoiling and losing nutritional value.

It is not only the insertion of new genes that concerns people. Deleting genes could also pose a health hazard. If scientists remove or inactivate a substance which they deem undesirable, the substance may have beneficial uses of which scientists are unaware or have little understanding. A good example

of these problems can be illustrated by data from the large amount of nutritional research being conducted. One of the difficulties scientists are having is that there often exist complex interactions. Determining whether a particular food component is harmful or damaging is contingent on what other components may be present or absent. Determining these complex interactions is frustrating to researchers. If we do not understand what a certain component does, how can we know the effects of adding or deleting it from a plant?

As humans, we eat a very diverse diet, so that any negative effects may be minimized. Domestic animals such as cattle, which rely on one or two crops such as corn, could be consuming large concentrations of toxins if they are present in the genetically engineered feed. These toxins, in turn, could affect the beef and poultry that we eat, as well as affecting other animals in the food chain. Birds and rodents could also eat the same engineered food material.

Wildlife could also be affected by plants which have been engineered to resist pests and diseases. The genetically altered plants could produce pollen or seeds that could flow to other wild or related plants. There is already a concern that genes for oilseed rape will influence wild mustards, which are a close relative. No one knows how new genetically engineered plants could affect the ecosystem.

Laws could be passed that would require growers to label any fruit or vegetable that came from a genetically altered plant. This could decrease the value of a crop in an area where genetic concerns, whether proven or not, have been raised.

There are many other concerns, such as side effects of genetic modification resulting in foods with diminished nutritional value. New proteins could cause hypersensitive or allergic reactions. One of the biggest concerns is that the effects could be gradual and take years, even decades, to show themselves.

No one knows the future of genetically altered foods. Some of it is available, and pressure for laws to label the products has by and large been unsuccessful. There could be a backlash against such products, but this can only happen if there is an awareness of the possible problems. The growth in scientifically altered and produced foods by large agribusinesses could create a backlash that could make natural, organic foods a premium product once again. Organic foods are already fetching premium prices because of fears of pesticide residues.

Of course, not all research produces harmful or detrimental results. Agricultural research is not the exclusive domain of scientists. Private breeders and companies are engaged in research, as are hobbyists and individual growers. Some of the best newer material is coming from individuals who do not have to function under the stringent guidelines imposed by institutions engaged in research. They have more latitude to develop an improved cultivar for a niche area or market, whereas institutional programs usually could never justify the cost of such an endeavor. Because of this, new and improved crops are available that can give the small growers the edge they need.

The Changsha Mandarin is an example of a citrus tree that can be grown as far north as Oregon.
(Jerry Black, Oregon Exotic Nursery photo.)

The future has always been uncertain, but there is one thing you can count on when it comes to agriculture of any kind: There is likely to be change, and a lot of it. Most change gives rise to a renaissance of traditional thought. With so many new and improved varieties, some growers are finding success and a feeling of solace in growing reliable and dependable historic or heirloom varieties. No matter what results appear from the multitude of research projects, the science of growing is likely headed for some major changes.

Farming has also come under heavy regulation by government. Many growers feel there are too many socialist thinkers and bureaucrats telling them how to farm. These planners often think that they know what is best for the American people. Fortunately, we still live in a democracy. Unfortunately, the strength of democracy is in the participation of its people, and when there is complacency, special interest groups or socialists seem to set the agenda. The solution is to organize and participate. Support candidates on all levels that believe in your values and objectives. Let them know that if they veer from your wants, you will withdraw your support. Many nominations, meetings, primaries and even elections are turned by a handful of votes. The squeaky wheel gets the grease, so squeak up!

Our planet has produced food since the dawn of time, and will probably always continue to do so. No matter how poorly we seem to treat our planet, it always seems to rejuvenate itself. Remember that planet Earth has gone through many ice ages and other catastrophic events and has always rebounded. Perhaps the damage that we are doing now is miniscule compared to events of the past.

Your key to success is how well you manage your time and your food production. Unfortunately, one of the biggest dangers to agriculture and many other related enterprises is not the weather, but debt. Thomas Jefferson once said that "Banking establishments are more dangerous than standing armies." If you owe little or no money, you have eliminated many factors that could interrupt your plans for self-sufficiency. In good years, put away capital. In poor years be frugal. In all years, rejoice in your harvest and enjoy a lifestyle for which many people yearn but few will ever experience.

All-America Selection winner Pumpkin Baby Bear.
(All-America Selection photo.)

If I had to sum up the principles of this book in a phrase, it would be to structure your growing by using common sense. The information and material to do so is readily available. Don't put all your eggs in one basket, and have respect for Mother Nature and the earth. After that, design a plan that is consistent with your objectives, and then initiate it. Remember, take care of your piece of the earth and it will take care of you.

Recommended Reading

Greening the Garden: A Guide to Sustainable Growing by Dan Jason. New Society Publishers, 1991, ISBN 0-86571-227-1. The theme of this gardening book is sustaining the earth through better gardening practices. The book also has much useful information, such as growing high protein plants, growing cover crops, and crop rotation.

Appendix

Gardening Book Sources

There are a number of presses that specialize in gardening and related books. It is a wise idea to get their catalogs (some of which are free) so that you can see what information is available. Owing to the popularity of gardening and its growing number of participants, there are books on practically every aspect of growing.

Dover Publications, Inc.
31 East 2nd Street
Mineola, NY 11501
516-294-7000

This company republishes books that have gone out of print. Most of their books cost between $1 and $6. There are more than 5,000 titles available, on every topic imaginable. They have hundreds of books on rural topics and horticulture. When you write, ask for their *Nature Book Catalog*. You should also ask for the *Dover Complete Catalog of Books in All Fields.*

Llewellyn
P.O. Box 64383
St. Paul, MN 55164-0383
1-800-The-Moon

This company publishes several books on herbal healing and lunar gardening, as well as gardening almanacs.

Loompanics Unlimited
P.O. Box 1197
Port Townsend, WA 98368
1-800-380-2230

If you put any importance on self-sufficiency, security and being informed, this publisher and seller of hard-to-find topics and fascinating titles will provide you with a source of books difficult to find elsewhere. Their catalog also makes fascinating reading. The catalog costs $5 by mail order, but comes free with any book order.

Storey Garden Way Publishing
Pownal, VT 05261
1-800-827-8673

There are hundreds of books on all kinds of topics which are of interest to the gardener. Many books on building, starting businesses and using your harvests are available.

Timber Press, Inc.
133 S.W. Second Avenue, Suite 450
Portland, OR 97204
1-800-327-5680

Timber Press offers a wide selection of books for the amateur and professional grower. They have excellent books on plant propagation, greenhouse management and specialty gardening topics.

Used Gardening Book Sources

Some of the best gardening and horticulture books have gone out of print. These titles can often be found at some of the companies that specialize in selling used books. One of the advantages of these firms is that you can save a great deal of money by not paying full price. Don't forget that many libraries occasionally have book sales, as do other organizations. I have purchased some excellent gardening books at yard sales. Below are three sources for used horticultural books.

agAccess
P.O. Box 2008
Davis, CA 95617
916-756-7177

This company offers a wide selection of new and used books for the gardener and the farmer. Many hard-to-find books, as well as text books, are available.

Brooks Books
P.O. Box 21473
Concord, CA 94521
510-672-4566

Each catalog contains hundreds of used books. This company specializes in books on botany and ornamental horticulture. They are a member of the Bookbytes out-of-print book network so that they can search via computer for books they do not have in stock.

Pomona Book Exchange
P.O. Box 111
Rockton, Ontario, Canada, L0R 1X0
519-621-8897

One of the best sources for out-of-print and used books on fruit growing. Titles on every aspect of horticulture are also carried.

Highly Recommended Reading

Gardening By Mail: Fourth Edition — Updated and Revised by Barbara J. Barton. Published by Houghton Mifflin Company, 215 Park Avenue South, New York, NY, 10003, 1994, ISBN: O-395-68079-4, 375 pages, indexes, 8½ x 11, softcover, $ 16.95.

This is the fourth edition of *Gardening by Mail* and as far as I am concerned, this book should be on every gardener's shelf! The book lists more than 1,000 seed companies and nurseries. There are also sections on horticultural societies, magazines, libraries and books. There is a massive index, so that once the reader finds what he needs, he can then look up the corresponding companies. Sources are also listed geographically so that the reader can quickly see which resources are nearest. This book has been presented with the highest award for General Gardening Books by the Garden Writers of America.

Finding & Buying Your Place in the Country — 3rd Edition by Les Scher & Carol Scher. Published by Dearborn Financial Publishing, Inc., 520 North Dearborn Street, Chicago, IL, 60610-4354, 1992, ISBN: 0-79310-395-9, 411 pages, Numerous charts and tables, 80 illustrations, sample contracts & deeds, index, 5 appendices, glossary, 8.5 x 11 softcover, $24.95.

Anyone who has contemplated buying a piece of land should have a copy of *Finding & Buying Your Place in the Country*. Probably the most comprehensive "Bible" on finding & buying your place in the country, this book contains thousands of items that will save anyone purchasing rural land hundreds, if not thousands of dollars, as well as saving time.

The book has 10 parts and thirty-four chapters. Some of the chapters are: Looking For Land, Checking out the Land, The Land and the Law (Chapters 8-18), Financing, Contract of Sale, Going Through Escrow and Using a Lawyer.

Finding & Buying Your Place in the Country will teach you how to test for groundwater pollution, how to use a lawyer, how to deal with real estate brokers, how to read a real estate ad, how to evaluate a house, as well as give you ample information on mineral, oil, gas, soil, water, easement and other rights, property taxes, zoning, deeds, contracts, insurance and loans.

The book was written by Les Scher, a lawyer who has specialized in country property for more than twenty years. Through his seminars, he has helped thousands of people buy country property. Carol Scher is a writer and consumer advocate.

Finding & Buying Your Place in the Country has already sold over 200,000 copies in the previous editions. These received rave reviews from *The New York Times*, *Chicago Tribune* and *Outside* magazine, just to name a few. This book is not just for those who want to avoid potential nightmares, but also for those who want to lower the cost and complexity of buying rural land or a rural home. People who already own country land will also benefit, and can consider this book an operating manual to deal with hundreds of interesting "country" problems that may occur from time to time.

Gardening Magazines and Newsletters

There are numerous gardening magazines and newsletters. Some of the smaller regional ones should not be overlooked since the majority of their information will probably apply to your gardening needs. Below are some of the magazines that I have found particularly useful and will help anyone to become more self-sufficient through gardening.

Backwoods Home Magazine
1267 Siskiyou Blvd, # 213
Ashland, OR 97520

This is the "practical journal of self reliance." Most of this magazine is written by real people with real experiences and not an editorial staff in New York, as is the case with many magazines. The publisher will not even consider an article unless it is practical, useful and understandable, and will entertain and educate the reader to be more self-sufficient.

The Business of Herbs
Northwind Farm Publications
Route 2, Box 246
Shevlin, MN 56676

This newsletter is excellent for those who grow herbs with the objective of earning money from them.

The Growing Edge Magazine
P.O. Box 1027
Corvallis, OR 97339

This magazine is for the advanced gardener, and has a focus on hydroponic and greenhouse gardening and new gardening technology.

Maine Organic Farmer & Gardener
P.O. Box 2176
Augusta, ME 04228

Not just for organic gardeners in the New England states, this publication is full of useful information applicable to other areas.

The Natural Farmer
411 Sheldon Road
Barre, MA 01005

This is the publication of the Northeast Organic Farming Association.

Organic Gardening
33 East Minor Street
Emmaus, PA 18098

The largest circulation of any organic-gardening magazine, this publication is a useful guide, especially for those new to gardening.

Rural Delivery
P.O. Box 1509
Liverpool, Nova Scotia, Canada B0T 1K0

The publisher and editor of this magazine wrote the best-selling books *The Family Cow* and *Small-Scale Pig Raising* (Storey Communications, Inc.). This down-to-earth magazine is full of practical advice.

Rural Heritage
281 Dean Ridge Lane
Gainsboro, TN 38562-9685

This magazine is dedicated to preserving the traditional rural lifestyle, and contains much practical information, particularly when it comes to working with horses.

Small Farmer's Journal
P.O. Box 2805
Eugene, OR 97402

For the small farmer, particularly those who work with horses. A wealth of information.

The Twenty-First Century Gardener
Grower's Press Inc.
P.O. Box 189
Princeton, British Columbia, Canada V0X 1W0

A well respected publication for greenhouse and hydroponic growers and those interested in the latest techniques available.

Associations & Organizations

My gardening has definitely benefited tremendously because I have used various organizations and their members to find information or procure plant material. Here are a few organizations worthy of consideration.

American Herb Association
P.O. Box 1673
Nevada City, CA 95959

American Pomological Society
102 Tyson Building
University Park, PA 16802

California Rare Fruit Growers, Inc.
P.O. Box W
El Cajon, CA 92022

Herb Research Foundation
1007 Pearl Street, Suite 200
Boulder, CO 80301

Heritage Seed Program
RR3
Uxbridge, Ontario, Canada L9P 1R3,

Hobby Greenhouse Association
18517 Kingshill Road
Germantown, MD 20874-2211

Hydroponic Society of America
P. O. Box 6067
Concord, CA 94524

National Hot Pepper Association
400 N.W. 20th Street
Ft. Lauderdale, FL 33311

North American Fruit Explorers
Route 1, Box 94
Chapin, IL 62628

Northern Nut Grower's Association
9870 S. Palmer Road
New Carlisle, OH 45344

Seed Savers Exchange
3076 North Winn Road
Decorah, IA 52101

Selected Seed Companies and Suppliers

There are thousands of sources available, and I strongly recommend the book *Gardening by Mail* mentioned earlier in the Appendix so that you can find many sources for the seeds, plants and other material or information you may need. Below are a few establishments that I have found to be reliable suppliers of high-quality and hard-to-find material.

W. Atee Burpee Company
300 Park Avenue
Warminster, PA 18974

This company has been offering seeds and other supplies since 1876. Good selection, catalog twice per year.

Edible Landscaping
P.O. Box 77
Afton, VA 22920

A good source for a wide selection of fruit trees, bushes and berries.

Fungi Perfecti
P.O. Box 7634
Olympia, WA 98507

This company offers mushroom growing kits and books for the mushroom grower.

Horticultural Enterprises
P.O. Box 810082
Dallas, TX 75381-0082

Mexican herbs and spices, plus a wide selection of sweet and chile peppers.

Johnny's Selected Seeds
Foss Hill Road
Albion, ME 04910-9731

One of my favorite catalogs, Johnny's has seeds for short seasons and carries rarely seen items such as grains. Not just for Northern growers.

New York State Fruit Testing
  Cooperative Association
P.O. Box 462
Geneva, NY 14456-0462

This association costs $5 to join and allows members to buy a large selection of fruit varieties. Highly recommended.

Oregon Exotics Rare Fruit Nursery
1065 Messinger Road
Grants Pass, OR 97527

By sending $2, you will get their catalog of rare and unique fruits, herbs and other edible plants from around the globe. This nursery has introduced over 100 new food varieties to North America from China, Russia, Nepal and other areas. Also highly recommended.

Park Seed Company, Inc.
P. O. Box 46
Highway 254 North
Greenwood, SC 29648-0046

This company has a very large selection of seeds and supplies.

Stark Brothers Nurseries & Orchards Co.
P. O. Box 10
Louisiana, MO 63353-0010

Since 1816 this company has been selling fruit trees, grapes and other plant material. Always something of interest.

Stokes Seed Company
P. O. Box 548
Buffalo, NY 14240

A wide selection of seeds for both commercial growers and gardeners. Many unique varieties that are exclusive from Stokes' respected breeding program.

Thompson & Morgan
P. O. Box 1308
Jackson, NJ 08527-0308

The catalog has a wide selection of unique and high-performance vegetables, many of which are from the United Kingdom.

The Tomato Seed Company, Inc.
P.O. Box 1400
Tyron, NC 28782

Over 300 varieties of tomato seeds. If you can't find the tomato you're looking for here, you probably won't find it.

Index

You Will Also Want To Read:

☐ **14133 THE HYDROPONIC HOT HOUSE, Low-Cost, High-Yield Greenhouse Gardening,** *by James B. DeKorne.* An illustrated guide to alternative-energy greenhouse gardening. Includes directions for building several different greenhouses, practical advice on harnessing solar energy, and many hard-earned suggestions for increasing plant yield. This is the first easy-to-use guide to home hydroponics. *1992, 5½ x 8½, 178 pp, illustrated, index, soft cover.* **$16.95.**

☐ **14193 BACKYARD MEAT PRODUCTION,** *by Anita Evangelista.* If you're tired of paying ever-soaring meat prices, and worried about unhealthy food additives and shoddy butchering techniques, then you should start raising small meat-producing animals at home! You needn't live in the country, as most urban areas allow for this practice. This book clearly explains how to raise rabbits, chickens, quail, pheasants, guineas, ducks, and mini-goats and -pigs for their meat and by-products, which can not only be consumed but can also be sold or bartered to specialized markets. Improve your diet while saving money and becoming more self-sufficient! *1997, 5½ x 8½, 136 pp, illustrated, soft cover.* **$14.95.**

☐ **14176 HOW TO DEVELOP A LOW-COST FAMILY FOOD-STORAGE SYSTEM,** *by Anita Evangelista.* If you're weary of spending a large percentage of your income on your family's food needs, then you should follow this amazing book's numerous tips on food-storage techniques. Slash your food bill by over fifty percent, and increase your self-sufficiency at the same time through alternative ways of obtaining, processing and storing foodstuffs. Includes methods of freezing, canning, smoking, jerking, salting, pickling, krauting, drying, brandying and many other food-preservation procedures. *1995, 5½ x 8½, 120 pp, illustrated, indexed, soft cover.* **$10.00.**

☐ **14187 HOW TO LIVE WITHOUT ELECTRICITY — AND LIKE IT,** *by Anita Evangelista.* There's no need to remain dependent on commercial electrical systems for your home's comforts and security. This book describes many alternative methods that can help one become more self-reliant and free from the utility companies. Learn how to light, heat and cool your home, obtain and store water, cook and refrigerate food, and fulfill many other household needs without paying the power company! *1997, 5½ x 8½, 168 pp, illustrated, soft cover.* **$13.95.**

Check out the catalog ad at the end of the book for the very best in controversial and unusual books. The catalog sells for $5. However, if you order any book from the following pages you will receive it *free* with your order. Also check out our web site at: www.loompanics.com.

SSG98

Loompanics Unlimited
PO Box 1197
Port Townsend, WA 98368

Please send me the books I have checked above. I have enclosed $_____ plus $4.95 for shipping and handling of books totaling $25.00. (Please add $1 for each additional $25 ordered.) Washington residents include 7.9% sales tax.

Name _____

Address _____

City/State/Zip _____

VISA and MasterCard accepted. 1-800-380-2230 for credit card orders only.
8am to 4pm, PST, Monday through Friday.

You Will Also Want To Read:

☐ **14178 THE WILD AND FREE COOKBOOK with a Special Roadkill Section,** *by Tom Squier.* Why pay top dollar for grocery-store food, when you can dine at no cost by foraging and hunting? Wild game, free of the steroids and additives found in commercial meat, is better for you, and many weeds and wild plants are more nutritious than the domestic fruits and vegetables found in the supermarket. Authored by a former Special Forces survival school instructor, this cookbook is chockfull of easy-to-read recipes that will enable you to turn wild and free food (including roadkill!) into gourmet meals. *1996, 7¼ x 11½, 306 pp, illustrated, indexed, soft cover.* **$19.95.**

☐ **14181 EAT WELL FOR 99¢ A MEAL,** *by Bill and Ruth Kaysing.* Want more energy, more robust, vigorous health? Then you must eat food that can impart these well-being characteristics and this book will be your faithful guide. As an important bonus, you will learn how to save lots of money and learn how to enjoy three homemade meals for a cost of less than one dollar per meal. The book will show you how to shop, how to stock your pantry, where to pick fresh foods for free, how to cook your 99¢ meal, what foods you can grow yourself, how to preserve your perishables, several recipes to get you started, and much much more. *1996, 5½ x 8½, 204 pp, illustrated, indexed, soft cover.* **$14.95.**

☐ **14183 THE 99¢ A MEAL COOKBOOK,** *by Ruth and Bill Kaysing.* Ruth and Bill Kaysing have compiled these recipes with one basic thought in mind: people don't like over-processed foods and they can save a lot of money by taking things into their own hands. These are practical recipes because they advise the cook where to find the necessary ingredients at low cost. And every bit as important — the food that you make will taste delicious! This is a companion volume to the *Eat Well for 99¢ A Meal.* Even in these days when the price of seemingly everything is inflated beyond belief or despair, 99¢ can go a long way toward feeding a person who is willing to save money by providing the labor for processing food. *1996, 5½ x 8½, 272 pp, indexed, soft cover.* **$14.95.**

Check out the catalog ad at the end of the book for the very best in controversial and unusual books you will find anywhere. The catalog sells for $5. However, if you order any book from the following pages you will receive it *free* with your order. Also check out our web site at: www.loompanics.com.

SSG98

Loompanics Unlimited
PO Box 1197
Port Townsend, WA 98368

Please send me the books I have checked above. I have enclosed $_____ plus $4.95 for shipping and handling of books totaling $25.00. (Please add $1 for each additional $25 ordered.) Washington residents include 7.9% sales tax.

Name_____

Address_____

City/State/Zip_____

VISA and MasterCard accepted. 1-800-380-2230 for credit card orders only.
8am to 4pm, PST, Monday through Friday.

You Will Also Want To Read:

You Will Also Want To Read:

☐ **13077 HOW TO MAKE CASH MONEY SELLING AT, SWAP MEETS, FLEA MARKETS, ETC.,** *by Jordan L. Cooper.* You can make money selling at swap meets, flea markets, etc. — once in a while as a part-time income, or as a full-time business. After years of making good money at flea markets, the author lets you in on the secrets of success. His tips and how-to's were learned from the School of Hard Knocks and can save you some hard knocks of your own. Topics covered include: What to Sell; Transportation; Setting-Up; How to Display Your Wares; Pricing; Saving Money on Food; Advertising; Rain and Bad Weather; The IRS; And much more. A low initial investment is all that's required, you can still hold your regular job while getting started, and you will be your own boss. *1988, 5½ x 8½, 180 pp, illustrated, soft cover.* **$16.95.**

☐ **64167 SECOND-HAND SUCCESS: How to Turn Discards into Dollars,** *by Jordan L. Cooper.* This is the story of successful people who turn discards into dollars. Jordan L. Cooper reveals the tricks used by dozens of clever entrepreneurs to turn trash into treasures. Learn where to find all kinds of used merchandise and where to sell it for top dollar. Topics covered include: Sources of Supply; Tips on Merchandising; Swap Meet Survival; Used Clothing; Small Appliances & Household Goods; Paperback Books; Used Cars; Seasonal Merchandise; Antiques & Collectibles; Arts & Crafts from Junque; Restoration; Handling Problems; And Much More! *1995, 5½ x 8½, 196 pp, illustrated, soft cover.* **$14.95.**

☐ **64145 $HADOW MERCHANT$, Successful Retailing Without a Storefront,** *by Jordan L. Cooper.* How to make money in low-overhead, street corner-style operations by someone who's been there. Covers: Swap Meets, Flea Markets; Street Corners; Arts & Crafts Shows; Mall Kiosks; Fairs & Carnivals; Gun Shows; Special Interest Events; And Much More! Also includes valuable advice on pitfalls to avoid. Shadow businesses are highly mobile, low-cost, low-risk operations that can be started without giving up your regular job. Many of the world's most famous businesses started out this way. The next success story could be yours. *1993, 5½ x 8½, 152 pp, illustrated, soft cover.* **$12.95.**

Check out the catalog ad at the end of the book for the very best in controversial and unusual books you will find anywhere. The catalog sells for $5. However, if you order any book from the following pages you will receive it *free* with your order. Also check out our web site at: www.loompanics.com.

SSG98

**Loompanics Unlimited
PO Box 1197
Port Townsend, WA 98368**

Please send me the books I have checked above. I have enclosed $_____ plus $4.95 for shipping and handling of books totaling $25.00. (Please add $1 for each additional $25 ordered.) Washington residents include 7.9% sales tax.

Name_____

Address_____

City/State/Zip_____

VISA and MasterCard accepted. 1-800-380-2230 for credit card orders only.
8am to 4pm, PST, Monday through Friday.

You Will Also Want To Read:

☐ **13063 SURVIVAL BARTERING, *by Duncan Long.*** People barter for different reasons — to avoid taxes, obtain a better lifestyle, or just for fun. This book foresees a time when barter is a necessity. Three forms of barter; Getting good deals; Stockpiling for future bartering; Protecting yourself from rip-offs; And much more. Learning how to barter could be the best insurance you can find. *1986, 5½ x 8½, 56 pp, soft cover.* **$8.00.**

☐ **17054 HOW TO BUY LAND CHEAP, Fifth Edition, *by Edward Preston.*** This is the bible of bargain-basement land buying. The author bought 8 lots for a total sum of $25. He shows you how to buy good land all over the country for not much more. This book has been revised, with updated addresses and new addresses added. This book will take you through the process for finding cheap land, evaluating and bidding on it , and closing the deal. Sample form letters are also included to help you get started and get results. You can buy land for less than the cost of a night out — this book shows how. *1996, 5½ x 8½, 136 pp, illustrated, soft cover.* **$14.95.**

☐ **14192 HOUSES TO GO, How To Buy A Good Home Cheap, *by Robert L. Williams.*** Now you can own that dream home that you've always yearned for — and at an affordable price! How? By following this book's tried-and-true method of purchasing a perfectly livable house that is destined for demolition, and carefully moving it to a suitable parcel of land where it can be mounted on a new foundation and adequately remodeled — all for a fraction of the amount such a home would normally cost! The author has done so several times, and shares his copious knowledge. Follow the process from selecting the proper house, through choosing a mover, to revamping the resettled house. Lots of photographs, and many solid tips on how to go about owning a valuable, comfortable home inexpensively. *1997, 8½ x 11, 152 pp, illustrated, soft cover.* **$18.95.**

☐ **14185 HOW TO BUILD YOUR OWN LOG HOME FOR LESS THAN $15,000, *by Robert L. Williams.*** When Robert L. Williams' North Carolina home was destroyed by a tornado, he and his family taught themselves how to construct a log home, even though they were unfamiliar with chain-saw construction techniques. In this practical, money-saving book, he clearly explains every step of the process. By following Williams' simple procedures, you can save tens, even hundreds of thousands of dollars, while building the rustic house you've always dreamed of owning! Profusely illustrated with diagrams and over 100 photographs, this is the best log-home construction book ever written. *1996, 8½ x 11, 224 pp, illustrated, soft cover.* **$19.95.**

Check out the catalog ad at the end of the book for the very best in controversial and unusual books you will find anywhere. The catalog sells for $5. However, if you order any book from the following pages you will receive it *free* with your order. Also check out our web site at: www.loompanics.com.

SSG98

Loompanics Unlimited
PO Box 1197
Port Townsend, WA 98368

Please send me the books I have checked above. I have enclosed $_____ plus $4.95 for shipping and handling of books totaling $25.00. (Please add $1 for each additional $25 ordered.) Washington residents include 7.9% sales tax.

Name _____

Address _____

City/State/Zip _____

VISA and MasterCard accepted. 1-800-380-2230 for credit card orders only.
8am to 4pm, PST, Monday through Friday.